APOCALYPSE

APOCALYPSE
A Catholic Perspective on the Book of Revelation

STEPHEN C. DOYLE, O.F.M.

ST. ANTHONY MESSENGER PRESS

Cincinnati, Ohio

RESCRIPT

In accord with the *Code of Canon Law*, I hereby grant my permission to publish *Apocalypse: A Catholic Perspective on the Book of Revelation* by Stephen C. Doyle, O.F.M.

Most Reverend Daniel E. Pilarczyk
Archbishop of the Archdiocese of
Cincinnati
Cincinnati, Ohio
June 9, 2005

The permission to publish is a declaration that a book or pamphlet is considered to be free from doctrinal or moral error. It is not implied that those who have granted the permission to publish agree with the contents, opinions or statements expressed.

Scripture passages have been taken from *New Revised Standard Version Bible,* copyright ©1989 by the Division of Christian Education of the National Council of the Churches of Christ in the U.S.A., and used by permission. All rights reserved.

Cover design by Eric Walljasper
Book design by Mark Sullivan

Library of Congress Cataloging-in-Publication Data

Doyle, Stephen C.
  Apocalypse : a Catholic perspective on the book of Revelation / Stephen C. Doyle.
    p. cm.
  Includes bibliographical references (p.   ) and index.
  ISBN 0-86716-571-5 (pbk. : alk. paper) 1. Bible. N.T. Revelation—Criticism, interpretation, etc. 2. Catholic Church—Doctrines. I. Title.

BS2825.52.D69 2005
228'.077—dc22

                                                            2005017073

ISBN 0-86716-571-5
Copyright ©2005, Stephen C. Doyle. All rights reserved.
Published by St. Anthony Messenger Press.
28 W. Liberty St.
Cincinnati, OH 45202
www.AmericanCatholic.org

Printed in the United States of America
Printed on acid-free paper

05 06 07 08 09 5 4 3 2 1

CONTENTS

INTRODUCTION

Like most people who are lovers of God's Word, for a long time, I was very uncomfortable with the Book of Revelation. I knew that on those rare occasions that it is part of the liturgical readings, the lector concludes with "Word of the Lord," just as with every other reading in the lectionary. And I had no doubt that it is the Word of the Lord, on a par with every other book in the Bible. But the problem for me was that it was so different from any other reading in the lectionary. It seemed to have little kinship with everything else that we called the Word of the Lord, especially in the New Testament.

I was used to going to the Bible for comfort and consolation, and even challenge and confrontation, but the Apocalypse, as it is known from the Greek, was more often confusing, disturbing, discouraging and even frightening. I just could not get clear what God, whom Jesus revealed as Father and whom John clearly insists is Love itself, was trying to tell us with such fantastic language and bizarre imagery ("So we have known and believe in the love that God has for us. God is love, and those who abide in love, abide in God, and God abides in them" [1 John 4:16]).

For one, the problem was compounded by those Christians who found the message of the Apocalypse to be self-evident. For them it was a clear-cut revelation of God's plan for today, requiring only a little wisdom to interpret. They treated it like the itinerary of the divine travel agent. Modern calamities and disasters were only stops on the itinerary, and matching them to a passage of the Apocalypse would give certain indication of where we are on the journey to the end of the world, the coming of God's Kingdom, and above all to the Parousia or second coming of Jesus.

I envied such certainty, for I prayed for God's Kingdom to come every time I prayed the Our Father. Jesus told me that that was the way he wanted me to pray. However, I found that every commentary on Revelation that told me exactly when Jesus would come again quickly had to be published in a second revised edition when the date passed and the predicted Parousia of Jesus did not happen. Those who simplistically treated the book as a crystal ball in which God was unveiling (that's what *revelation* means) the details of future history did not seem to have any more of a clue to its meaning than I did.

But I found that there was a way out of the confusion, a way to hear what God was saying, a means of interpreting the book in the way that God intended. Twenty years before the Second Vatican Council, in 1943, Pope Pius XII had provided the means and direction for interpreting God's Word as God wanted it to be understood. Following his directives, the Book of Revelation not only finally made sense but also proved to be a gold mine for spirituality and evangelization.

The pope's directives were reaffirmed twenty years later by the Second Vatican Council in 1965 which, in its *Constitution on Divine Revelation,* further opened the doors for us to be a biblical church. The directives are three:

1. Go back to the original languages in which God spoke to us through the human author.
2. Find out what that human author intended to say.
3. Determine the literary form or kind of literature that the author used to convey God's message in human language.

THE ORIGINAL LANGUAGES

In the Bible, God spoke to us in the languages of the people: Hebrew and Aramaic in the Old Testament, and Greek in the New Testament. When scholars studied the Apocalypse, they found that the author thought in Aramaic, the language of Jesus (Hebrew is a derivative of it, as Italian is of Latin), but used Greek words. If you have ever run into an immigrant who speaks English while thinking in his native language, you get the picture. We call it broken English.

The author of Revelation used "broken Greek"! That tells us something about him. He came from Palestine, the land of Jesus, where Aramaic was spoken. But his readers dwelt in an area where Greek, not his native Aramaic, was spoken. He identifies the place where he is writing as the island of Patmos, many miles from Aramaic-speaking Palestine, but just off the coast of Greek-speaking Asia Minor.

Examining the text in the original language has also shown us that almost two-thirds of the book is implicit quotes from the Old Testament (also called the Hebrew Scriptures). The author quotes his Bible from memory, not using exact quotations but as if it were a part of him and his spirituality. This, among other things, has led people to say that this book is more like an Old Testament book than a New Testament one. That is to say that the teaching and spirituality that Jesus calls us to advances that of the Old Testament (cf. the Sermon on the Mount: "It was said to you of old...but I say to you" [Matthew 5:21, 27, 31, 33, 38, 43]).

Many of the teachings of this Christian book, however, seem to remain at the level of the Hebrew Scriptures. Jesus' preaching and spirituality in all of their depth and richness do not seem to be as fully reflected in this book as in other books of the New Testament. But every book, whether epistle, gospel or Apocalypse, has its limitations and cannot say everything. So to point out where the Book of Revelation is limited is not to dismiss it. We must recognize its limitations and also recognize that it is God's Word, "broken Greek" and all.

THE INTENTION OF THE AUTHOR

Perhaps more than any other book of the Bible, the Book of Revelation has been the victim of people reading their own ideas into it rather than listening to what the author intended to say. If I am to grasp what you are trying to say to me, I must know something about you, how you think, how you approach problems, your view of life, what makes you tick and, in particular, what problem you are trying to solve or what question you are trying to answer. Remember that God's Word is usually the solution to a problem or the answer to a question.

In the Bible we have the solution and the answer. We have to do a little bit of work to find out what was the problem or the question. That is why it is so important to know the culture, civilization and history that are part of the author. They are the stage from which he speaks. And he is speaking primarily to his own time, not to ours. It is only when we find out what he meant to say to his contemporaries that we can find out what he has to say to us today.

THE LITERARY FORM

When we go to the library or to a bookstore looking for a book, we must know what kind of literary form it is or we will never find it. Novels will not be found in the section for history books, and political essays are not catalogued among joke books. Nor are hymnbooks on the same shelf with political satire, and books of poetry are not mixed with how-to books. Each literary form—even cartoons, jokes and poetry—can convey truth. But we will miss the truth if we mistake the literary form.

The Bible itself, often called a book, is really a library. It is a collection of books with a variety of ancient literary forms, some of which are no longer familiar to us. Among the most unfamiliar of them is the literary form called Apocalypse. Before examining the characteristics of this unique literary form it should not be forgotten that the entire Bible, not just one book, is a revelation from God.

The Second Vatican Council stated:

> In His goodness and wisdom, God chose to reveal Himself and to make known to us the hidden purpose of his will (cf. Eph. 1:9) by which through Christ, the Word made flesh, we have access to the Father in the Holy Spirit and come to share in the divine nature (cf. Eph. 2:18; 2 Pet. 1:4). Through this *revelation*, therefore, the invisible God (cf. Col. 1:15; 1 Tim. 1:17) out of the abundance of his love, speaks to us as friends (cf. Ex.33:11; Jn 15:14–15) and lives among them (cf. Bar. 3:38) so that he might invite and take us into fellowship with himself. This plan of *revelation* is realized by deeds and words having an inner unity: The deeds wrought by God in the history of salvation manifest and confirm the teaching and realities signified by the words, while the words proclaim the deeds and clarify the mystery contained in them. By this *revelation,* the deepest truth about God and our salvation is made clear to us in Christ, who is the mediator and at the same time the fullness of all *revelation. (Constitution on Divine Revelation,* 2, emphasis added)

Notice that the Council tells us that all "revelation" reveals to us God's presence, friendship and fellowship (union or communion) with himself. That includes the Book of Revelation, and that is why, like all the other books of the Bible, it is a resource for spirituality and evangelization.

In the opening line of this, the last book of the Bible, the author not only tells us that this is a message from God, part of his "revelation," but it is also a kind of literature or literary form called "Revelation" (in Greek, *apocalypse*). It is not very familiar to us but if we were to go into a library over nineteen hundred years ago at the time of our author, we would find a whole shelf full of "apocalypses."

Their main characteristics are:

1. They are crisis literature.

These works were tracts for hard times, written in an era of terrible tension and great suffering, when it seems that God's creation is reverting to chaos. It appears that the forces of evil have the upper hand and the believer is confused. Where is God in this horror show?

2. They rely on symbolism.

The author's writing is disloyal and even treasonable to the existing political order because it is encroaching on God's power. Therefore he must use symbols that are easily understood by his audience, whom he is rousing to resistance and even revolt but appear to be the ravings of a lunatic should it fall into the hands of the civil authorities. Part of our problem today in reading him is our lack of familiarity with this kind of literature and the Hebrew Scriptures from which the symbols were taken. For him and his people, the Hebrew Scriptures were the only Bible, a book totally unfamiliar to their enemies. (And to many Christians today, unfortunately!)

3. They telescope time.

Key to the understanding of the intention of the author is to realize that part of his plan for the deception of the authorities is to take the events of the past as revealed in the Hebrew Scriptures and pretend that he is speaking about or revealing the future. His readers know what an apocalypse is and know what he is up to; they realize that he is really addressing the present crisis going on around them. He has no intention of predicting the future. He is trying to give them hope in the present. His message is not "pie in the sky, by and by" but that God is with them now, even when it does not seem so. When we have listened to his message to his contemporaries we may very well find that it sheds light on our chaotic times, not because he predicted events but because we are facing the same problems that he did, when once again governments so often encroach on the prerogatives of God: "The more things change, the more they remain the same."

Orientation and Methodology: Each chapter begins with a passage of the Book of Revelation from the *New Revised Standard Version*. This is followed by an explanation that attempts to elucidate the overarching truth conveyed in the passage. This is frequently done by the use of other quotes from the Old (Hebrew Scriptures) and New Testament, since the best commentary on the Bible is the Bible.

No effort has been made to elucidate every sign and symbol of the book. This would obfuscate the dominant themes and miss the forest for the trees. The bibliography contains works of excellent scholars where further study can be profitably done on individual symbols or passages.

Each chapter concludes with a reflection that casts light on the meaning of the text for today and/or provides further incentive to prayer and evangelization. These are taken from *The Documents of Vatican II*, Walter Abbott, S.J., ed., America Press, New York, 1966, and the *Decree on Evangelization* of Pope Paul VI, 1976, among other sources.

Note on Authorship: There is no consensus as to the identity of the author who calls himself "John, your brother." All other apocalypses, however, are written under a pseudonym of a great leader of the "good old days." This subterfuge provides anonymity from the persecutor and a higher authority for the work in the community.

One attractive theory is that of J.M. Ford in her commentary on the Book of Revelation in the Anchor Bible Series. In her hypothesis the work originated in the hellfire-and-brimstone preaching of John the Baptist (Matthew 3:7–11). He was the last of the Old Testament prophets

(Matthew 11:11). His movement did not die with him and his disciples were found as far away as Egypt, Ephesus and Corinth (Acts 18:4; 19:3; 1 Corinthians 1:12; 3:4; 4:6; 16:12 and Titus 3:13). In fact, communities of the Baptist's disciples have survived to this day in the mountain villages of Iraq.

His preaching was preserved and developed and applied to the life situation of the next generation. (This is similar to the development of the Gospels from the preaching of Jesus. Cf. the Pontifical Biblical Commission's document on the "Formation of the Gospels," 1964.) Then some of his followers came into the church and their traditions were Christianized by the community and developed, reflecting their own faith and experience, and finally resulting in the Book of Revelation.

The Essenes at Qumran produced a huge library, and their contemporaries—the Christians—produced the New Testament. Jesus frequently refers to the "traditions of the elders" of the Pharisees. It is not at all strange then that the widespread disciples of John the Baptist might have put down their own traditions to reflect their experience and catechize the next generation. This, however, is theory and not fact. We'll get the real story when we get to heaven!

REFLECTION

In sacred Scripture, without prejudice to God's truth and holiness, the marvelous condescension of eternal wisdom is plain to be seen that we may come to know the ineffable loving-kindness of God, and see for ourselves how far he has gone in adapting his language, with thoughtful concern, to our nature. Indeed, the words of God, expressed in the words of men are in every way like human language, just as the Word of the Eternal Father, when he took on himself the flesh of human weakness, became like us... (adapted from *Constitution on Divine Revelation*, 13).

CHAPTER ONE

PROLOGUE OF THE BOOK OF REVELATION (1:1–3)

The revelation of Jesus Christ which God gave to him to show his servants what must soon take place; he made it known by sending his angel to his servant John, who testified to the word of God and to the testimony of Jesus Christ, even to all that he saw.

Blessed is the one who reads aloud the words of the prophecy, and blessed are those who hear and who keep what is written in it; for the time is near.

This passage was not written by the author of the book, "John," but by another person who tells us what to expect in the book that we are about to read. He tells us three things:

1. It is a message to his servants right from the source, from God through Jesus Christ, which will enable those serving him (i.e., on the same wave length) to penetrate the veil of unfolding history and find its real meaning from God's viewpoint. It presumes that those who receive the message are followers, disciples, believers in Jesus. It is not a message for the movers and shakers of this world who think of themselves as the architects of history.

If the meaning of the acts and events of history were self-evident, they would not require a revelation. The author is saying that there is more here than meets the eye. Appearances are deceiving. Anyone with a bit of common sense is able to tell you what is *happening*. But *what is going on* can only be grasped by those who know who is really in charge, who is the Lord of history. If this were the stock market and not spirituality, we would call this revelation "insider trading," privileged information for those in the know, the friends of Jesus.

This also presumes that the believer has an advantage not available to the bystander or casual observer who might be led to despair over his helplessness in the present desperate situation. Because the believer knows that he is not in control of the situation, he can be a person of joyful heart: Things are in good hands, God's good hands.

The world may seem to be out of control, but it is not out of God's control! Thus this revelation is a cause for joy and optimism. "He's got the whole world in his hands!" is not just a nice folk song, it is the absolute truth and the fundamental theology of this book.

2. The serious reader of this book is called "blessed." It is the first of seven beatitudes in the book (cf. 14:13; 16:15; 19:9; 20:6; 22:7 and 14). In the Bible, to be blessed is to be one in whom the power and grace of God are evident. When Elizabeth said to Mary, "Blessed are you among women," she was really saying the same thing as the Angel Gabriel said: "Hail Mary, full of grace, the Lord is with you." To be blessed is to be a sign of the love and saving presence of God. The church beatifies people and tells us we can call them blessed because the serious person can detect that God was active in them, that their lives were miracles of God's grace. The miracle required for their beatification is a confirmation of what they already were in their lives among us. They were a revelation. They showed us God!

And the author tells us that we are numbered among them if we are willing to read aloud, hear and keep the words of this prophecy. It is to be read aloud, because it is intended for the community, the church gathered for worship. (More on that when we reach chapter four.) The injunction "to hear and keep" is reminiscent of the job description that Yahweh gave to his people through Moses at Sinai: "If you *obey* my *voice* and *keep* my covenant..." (Exodus 19:5). In Hebrew, the word for *to obey, shamah,* is also the word for *to hear*. The author could hardly have expressed in stronger language the importance of taking his message seriously.

He also tells us that this word, this message, falls into a special category of God's communications to his people: prophecy. It falls into the category of the messages that we have from Jesus, who was recognized as a prophet by the common people, if not by the religious professionals: "A great prophet has arisen among us" (Luke 7:16). And he proclaimed that he was one of the prophets when he was dismissed by the people of his hometown, Nazareth: "Truly, I tell you that no prophet is accepted in the prophet's hometown" (Luke 4:24). Many people today think of a prophet as one who predicts the future, which is why they miss the point of the prophetic message of the Book of Revelation. They are so busy trying to find out what the future holds that they miss what is going on in the present. Jesus did not predict the future except to tell people what the consequences would be if they did not repent.

Jesus knew his Bible. As a twelve-year-old he is depicted as discussing it with the experts in the temple. He knew that like the prophets of old, his Father had not sent him to allay peoples' fears about the future. He came to be "the way, the truth and the life" right now. As a prophet Jesus provided a model for those who would come after him in the church he founded. "Those who prophesy speak to other people for their upbuilding, encouragement and consolation....those who prophesy build up the church" (1 Corinthians 14:3–4).

In the very first, earliest New Testament document, Paul writes to the infant church of Thessalonica: "We appeal to you, brothers and sisters to respect those who labor among you, and have charge of you in the Lord and admonish you; esteem them very highly in love because of their work....Do not quench the Spirit. Do not despise the words of prophets." Saint Paul wrote that about fifteen years after Jesus' resurrection (1 Thessalonians 5:12, 20). Those who first heard the Book of Revelation recognized that it was in the great tradition of Jesus and of all his prophetic predecessors; for like them, it reminded the establishment what it was established for and comforted the afflicted and afflicted the comfortable.

3. "For the time is near!" is found right at the beginning of the book, and the last chapter insists: "The Lord, the God of the spirits of the prophets, has sent his angel to show his servants what must soon take place. See, I am coming soon. Blessed is the one who keeps the words of the prophecy of this book" (22:6–7). "Do not seal up the words of the prophecy of this book, for the time is near" (22:10). "See, I am coming soon, my reward is with me, to repay according to everyone's work" (22:12). "The one who testifies to these things says: "Surely I am coming soon. Amen, Come Lord Jesus" (22:20).

The author wants to create a sense of urgency. We who live nineteen centuries after this was written must recognize that "soon" and "the time is near" cannot refer to a time value of a few days, weeks, months or even years. They are meant to bring us to attention so that we will not be complacent. They impart a sense of immediacy as Jesus did in Mark's Gospel:

> But about that day or hour no one knows, neither the angels in heaven, nor the Son, but only the Father. Beware, keep alert; for you do not know when the time will come. It is like a man going on a journey, when he leaves home and puts his slaves in charge, each with his work, and commands the doorkeeper to be on the watch. Therefore, keep awake—for you do not know when the master of the house will come, in the evening, or at midnight, or at cockcrow, or at dawn, or else he may find you asleep when he comes suddenly. And what I say to you I say to all: Keep awake. (13:32–37)

If the message of this book of God's word is not primarily intended for the church at the end of the first century as an answer to their questions and a solution to their problems, then God is playing games and not to be taken seriously. But he does not play games and is to be taken seriously, and this book will tell us what solution he gave to their problems, what answer he gave to their questions. Then, because the Word of the Lord endures forever, we will find its relevance for our own times. If we know what those early Christians were facing then we will quickly perceive that the same "word of prophecy" that spoke to them is not a historical curiosity but a dynamic challenge that God is still sending to us. If we follow the author's advice and listen closely, we will hear what God is telling us today for our own spiritual life and evangelization.

The author may also accomplish something else, beyond his words, by being a role model. From his own age he reminds us that the church in every age needs prophets to remind the establishment what it was established for. And since prophets are critics of the status quo and consciences of the institution, they are not only unwelcome but their voices must also be stifled as disturbers of the peace. Accusing them of blasphemy against religion or disloyalty to the state is a good way to eliminate them. Just ask Jesus!

REFLECTION

It is an easy assumption that prophecy as a distinct function has ceased in the church or that the prophetic function has been subsumed into the official teaching office...It is obvious that the church needs prophets and has had prophets....Prophecy is the voice of the Spirit which speaks to the officers and members of the church when either officers or other members are unfaithful to their own charisma....The prophet is the means by which the Spirit protects the church against corruption, and it takes a prophet to point out that there are other means of corruption than concubinage, nepotism and simony. (John L. McKenzie, S.J., to the Catholic Biblical Association)

CHAPTER TWO

YOU ARE NOT ALONE (1:4–7)

John, to the seven churches that are in Asia: Grace to you and peace from him who is and who was and who is to come, and from the seven spirits who are before his throne, and from Jesus Christ, the faithful witness, the firstborn from the dead, and the ruler of the kings of the earth.

To him who loves us and freed us from our sins by his blood, and made us to be a kingdom, priests serving his God and Father, to him be glory and dominion forever and ever. Amen.

Look, He is coming with the clouds;
> every eye will see him,
even those who pierced him;
> and on his account all the tribes of the earth will wail.
So it is to be. Amen.

The next paragraph lists the names of all those seven churches of Asia Minor (present-day Turkey) and the next two chapters contain individual letters or epistles for each of them. However, the very fact that the church preserved this book and these letters tells us that here we have the Word of God. And the Word of God, which endures forever, is always an invitation not only to those to whom it was first addressed, but also to all peoples, everywhere and forever.

And like many invitations, it has an RSVP attached. Are you coming or not? It is the Lord who invites, and he won't take no for an answer. He wasn't just speaking to those ancient churches. He is speaking to the church today. The invitation may seem a bit garbled to us, but it was perfectly clear to the Christians of the first century. When we find out what it said to them, then we are well on our way to finding out what it says to us Christians of the twenty-first century. Only then can we respond to the invitation.

And this invitation is not just from anyone. It is from the eternal God in the fullness of his spiritual power (seven is fullness or perfection; cf. Isaiah 11:2) and the risen Jesus, who is Lord. It is he who "hands over the kingdom to God the Father, after he has destroyed every ruler and every authority and power. For he must reign until he has put all his enemies under his feet. The last enemy to be destroyed is death. For God has put all things in subjection under his feet...so that God may be all in all" (1 Corinthians 15:24–28). Quite an occasion we are being invited to, but it is no surprise party. We have been joined to the church at its very origin in praying for that invitation when we say "Thy Kingdom come, thy will be done."

In these, the very first lines of the book, the author shares the point of view of another author who wrote Hebrews: the church is a pilgrim. She has not arrived. She is in motion, and lest she lose her way she must keep her eye on her Lord who has gone before her, the leader of the pilgrimage. "We have this hope, a sure and steadfast anchor of the soul, a hope that enters the inner shrine behind the curtain [i.e., heavenly sanctuary] where Jesus, a forerunner [the leader of the pilgrimage] on our behalf, has entered, having become a high priest forever" (Hebrews 6:19–20). "Christ did not enter a sanctuary made by human hands....but he entered into heaven itself, now to appear in the presence of God on our behalf" (9:24). "And just as it is appointed for mortals to die once, and after that the judgment, so Christ, having been offered once to bear the sins of many, will appear a second time, not to deal with sin, but to save those who are eagerly waiting for him" (9:27).

Indeed, it is the very vision that Vatican II reclaimed when it declared that we are a pilgrim church: "Still in pilgrimage upon the earth, we trace in trial and under oppression the paths he trod. Made one with his sufferings, as the body is with the head, we endure with him, that with him we may be glorified" (*Constitution on the Church*, 7). This is repeated in a quote from Saint Augustine: "The Church 'like a pilgrim in a foreign land presses forward amid the persecution of the world, and the consolations of God, announcing the cross and death of the Lord until he comes'" (*Constitution on the Church*, 8).

But a pilgrimage can turn into a bit of meandering if the pilgrims don't keep their eye on the leader. Hope can turn to despair if we don't keep our eye on Jesus, if we don't have a vision, if we are not sustained by a clear view of our leader. "Look," says our author. "If you don't, you may get lost, for where he is we pilgrims are headed." A minister general of the Franciscan order, which is a microcosm of the whole church, said that the Lord has called us to be pilgrims and strangers in this world but too often we wind up being tourists and vagabonds!

Before the author of the Book of Revelation invites us to join Jesus on pilgrimage, he gives us a vivid portrait and vision of our leader so we will not lose sight of him: "Jesus Christ, the faithful witness, the firstborn from the dead, and the ruler of the kings of the earth. So it is to be, Amen."

REFLECTION

The [Second Vatican] Council envisages the Church as continuing the work of the Good Shepherd, who came to serve and not to be served, and who did not hesitate to lay down his life for his sheep. But the Church is represented very realistically as a "little flock" made up of frail and sinful men. Weak and humble, it stands in constant need of purification and renewal. At the same time, however, it feels confident of God's loving help which guides its steps. Throughout this constitution (*On the Church*), the mystery of the Church is viewed in terms of the paradoxical union between the human and the divine. Because the Church is human, it exists in time and is subjected to the forces of history. But because of its divine element, it presses forward full of optimism toward a goal beyond history. In all its prayers and labors, it is sustained by the glorious vision of the final kingdom in which God will be all in all. (Avery Dulles, S.J., in *Documents of Vatican II,* p. 11)

CHAPTER THREE

"LORD, GOD ALMIGHTY" (1:8)

I am the Alpha and the Omega, says the Lord God, who is and who was and who is to come, the Almighty.

The Greek word for *Almighty* as a title of God is *Pantocrator*. The author uses it frequently, nine times in this book. It comes from the Greek, meaning *ruler of all*. In the churches of the East this is a common name of God carried over into theology, spirituality and art. Since the architecture of the National Shrine of the Immaculate Conception in Washington, D.C., is derived from the Byzantine or Eastern style, high above the main altar in the apse is the Byzantine mosaic image of the *Pantocrator*. To convey the idea that Jesus is almighty, all-powerful, without peer or competitor, he is made to appear so stern, if not angry. There are those who feel the image would be more at home in the Pentagon. They have a point.

In the West, *Pantocrator* has not become part of our spiritual vocabulary, but we use synonyms, taken from Old Testament imagery: "Lord God Almighty, *Yahweh Sabaoth*, Lord of Hosts." This vocabulary is borrowed from military language. To say that God is "Lord of Hosts" or "Yahweh Sabaoth" is to say that he is commander-in-chief.

The force and power of the title may have been diminished by repetition, but as a response to the Preface of every Mass we proclaim that he is "Holy, Holy, Holy, Lord God of power and might." The previous translation proclaimed him "Lord of Hosts," which is the translation of *Yahweh Sabaoth*. This was one of the earliest and most common forms of address for God in the Hebrew Scriptures (used over 250 times!). God's people, besieged on every side by their enemies, had only to raise their eyes to behold the *Sabaoth*, the hosts, the heavenly powers, the "troops" of Yahweh, who was their commander-in-chief.

When Israel settled in the land, she was vulnerable to the attacks of the surrounding nations: Canaan, Philistia, Syria, Edom and Moab, to say nothing of the great empires to the north and south that were ready to pounce on her. In one of the earliest usages of the title, little David with his slingshot, challenges Goliath, the giant of the Philistines: "I come to you in the name of the Lord of Hosts, the God of the armies of Israel whom you have defied" (1 Samuel 17:45). He may have seemed to be alone and helpless, but almighty God in all of his power was with the lad. And David won! Or rather, the Lord of Hosts, the God of the armies of Israel, prevailed again on behalf of his people.

This military language of the commander-in-chief of the Israelite armed forces is carried even into the Bible's poetry and song. The second half of Psalm 24 (vv. 7–10) is a celebration of victory when *Yahweh Sabaoth* on the Ark of the Covenant aboard a wheeled cart returns from battle. At the portal of the temple a choir chants:

"Lift up your heads, O gates!
and be lifted up, O ancient doors!
That the King of glory may come in."
A second choir, within the temple, chants:
"Who is the King of glory?"
Then the first choir, accompanying the Ark, chants the reply:
"The LORD, strong and mighty,
the LORD, mighty in battle."
And they repeat the plea:
"Lift up your heads, O gates!
and be lifted up, O ancient doors!
that the King of glory may come in."
Then the refrain from within: "Who is this King of glory?" And as the entrance to the Holy of Holies, the throne room of Yahweh Sabaoth is opened to the resounding chorus:
"The LORD of hosts, / he is the King of glory."
(The Advent hymn, "The King of Glory comes, the nation rejoices" is derived from this passage.)

This concept of God as almighty creates a problem, however. If God is all-powerful, that does not leave room for anyone else to have any power. He has it all. And in order to show that he has it all, every other creature must be depicted as powerless, even without the power to make a choice. It is for this reason that so many stories narrated in the Old Testament show that there is no contest when Almighty God is involved. They make for some incredible, and sometimes amusing, reading. Chapters four and five of Exodus basically tell the story of God commissioning Moses to go to Pharaoh and tell him to let his people go. But then God says of the supposedly almighty ruler of Egypt: Before you get to him I am going to harden his heart so that he will not let my people go, and then I can punish him for having a hardened heart! Obviously, Pharaoh had not the slightest chance. And that is precisely the point when you are dealing with the Lord almighty!

No less than the first and perhaps greatest theologian of the church, Saint Paul, wrestled with the problem from a personal point of view. Based upon his own conversion experience, he came to believe that the Jewish people would convert to Jesus *en masse*. As he nears the end of his life and writes to the Romans in preparation for his arrival there, he is at a loss to figure out why his kindred have not followed in his footsteps. Is it because they have rejected outright the call of Christ? Or has God withheld from them the grace of conversion? Had God predestined them to be deprived of the saving grace of Jesus, or in their stubbornness had they opted and freely chosen to be without it, and thus outside of salvation?

In trying to reconcile God's omnipotence and the free will with which he endowed his creatures, Paul's reasoning becomes convoluted and confusing, and then when he tries to give an analogy to illustrate it, it falls flat on its face.

> You will say to me then, "Why then does he still find fault? For who can resist his will?" But who indeed are you, a human being, to argue with God? Will what is molded say to the one who molds it, "Why have you made me like this?" Has the potter no right over the clay, to make out of the same lump one object for special use and another for ordinary use? What if God, desiring to show his wrath and to make known his power, has endured with much

patience the objects of wrath that are made for destruction; and what if he has done so in order to make known the riches of his glory for the objects of mercy, which he has prepared beforehand for glory—including us whom he has called, not from the Jews only but also from the Gentiles?" (Romans 9:19–23)

But a lump of clay has neither intelligence nor free will. So much for the analogy!

In utter frustration, two chapters of close and intricate arguing later, Paul cries out:

O the depth of the riches and wisdom and knowledge of God! How unsearchable are his judgments and how inscrutable his ways!
"For who has known the mind of the Lord?
Or who has been his counselor?" (11:33–34)

Do we have a chance, or is God so in charge that everything is predestined? And if the latter is the case, are we not responsible, deserving of neither praise nor blame, reward nor punishment? We do have a chance. Obviously, the very fact that we have a Bible with God's inspired and inviting word is a sure sign that we can say yes or no, I will or I will not. And just how it can be that God is all powerful and yet he made us so that we can either cooperate with him or resist him is at the very heart of the mystery of free will. Theologians and spiritual writers have wrestled with the question for centuries. And when all is said and done, the mystery remains. We must avoid what has been called the occupational hazard of theologians: their inability to admit: "I don't know." What we do know is that Almighty God has given us the gift of free will. If he had not, we would not be able to love, and that is what his word calls us to.

REFLECTION

When the Son of Man comes in his glory, and all the angels with him, then he will sit on the throne of his glory. All the nations will be gathered before him, and he will separate people one from another as a shepherd separates the sheep from the goats, and he will put the sheep at his right hand and the goats at the left. Then the king will say to those at his right hand, "Come, you that are blessed by my Father, inherit the kingdom prepared for you from the foundation of the world; for I was hungry and you gave me food, I was thirsty and you gave me something to drink, I was a stranger and you welcomed me, I was naked and you gave me clothing, I was sick and you took care of me, I was in prison and you visited me...." (Matthew 25:31–36)

CHAPTER FOUR

YOUR BROTHER (1:9–11)

> I, John, your brother who share with you in Jesus the persecution
> and the kingdom and the patient endurance, was on the island
> called Patmos because of the word of God and the testimony of
> Jesus. I was in the spirit on the Lord's day, and I heard behind me
> a loud voice like a trumpet saying, "Write in a book what you see
> and send it to the seven churches, to Ephesus, to Smyrna, to
> Pergamum, to Thyatira, to Sardis, to Philadelphia, and to
> Laodicea.

Is this John the Evangelist, the Beloved Disciple, John the Theologian,
John the Baptist or another using the pseudonym John (cf. note on authorship on p. xiii)? Many books of the Bible are written under pseudonyms.
And all other apocalypses are written under the pseudonym of a famous
person like Moses or Enoch. Such anonymity gives a work a borrowed
authority and also saves the author from being known to the church's enemies. It is enough to know that the human author is our "brother." The
Greek word for *share* here (*koinonia*) is used in an intensive form. The
author's deep sharing with us is not because we all belong to the same
mutual fraternal organization or club. As Paul has told us thirty years
before this was written, our sharing is because we are the body of Christ.

The author of this book, not writing from an ivory tower, knows what
we are going through. He knows because he is carrying his own cross. He
is in a Roman penal colony on an isolated, waterless and barren island. He
is suffering because he is a witness (in Greek, *martyr*) to Jesus and his
gospel. That is what it takes to be a Christian! Jesus carried his cross and
warned that we could not be his disciples unless we carried ours. He calls
for "patient endurance" because just as surely as the cross was followed by
the Resurrection, their sharing in suffering will lead to their sharing in the
kingdom, which they have prayed for each time they called upon the
source of their sharing: "Our Father."

Whether penal colony or imperial persecution, he wants them to know that whatever cross they have, they are not in it alone. Christ has called them not only to suffering and death, but also resurrection and triumph.

> It is Christ Jesus, who died, yes, who was raised, who is at the right hand of God, who indeed intercedes for us. Who will separate us from the love of Christ? Will hardship, or distress, or persecution, or famine, or nakedness, or peril, or sword? As it is written:
>
> "For your sake we are being killed all day long;
> we are accounted as sheep to be slaughtered."
>
> No, in all these things we are more than conquerors through him who loved us. For I am convinced that neither death, nor life, nor angels, nor rulers, nor things present, nor things to come, nor powers, nor height, nor depth, nor anything else in all creation, will be able to separate us from the love of God in Christ Jesus our Lord. (Romans 8:34–39)

Cross and resurrection, sacrifice and exaltation, suffering and triumph, struggle and victory, martyrdom and crown, persecution and vindication, slavery and redemption: These are two sides of the same coin. We will not have one without the other, because the disciple is not greater than the Master.

It is the proclamation of this mystery that a heavenly voice commands Paul to share with seven communities on the mainland. This is not just because they are united in suffering but also because they are "church." His Greek word *ekklesia* is from *ek,* meaning "out from" and *kaleo,* meaning "call." They are Christians because they have been called out from isolation, self-pity, trying to save themselves, self-centeredness and futility. They have been called to be sharers, church, the body of Christ. That is the reason for which he was arrested. But even prison did not silence him. He is still the sharer and bearer of the Good News.

REFLECTION

The gifts he gave were that some would be apostles, some prophets, some evangelists, some pastors and teachers, to equip the saints for the work of ministry, for building up the body of Christ, until all of us come to the unity of the faith and of the knowledge of the Son of God, to maturity, to the measure of the full stature of Christ. We must no longer be children, tossed to and fro and blown about by every wind of doctrine, by people's trickery, by their craftiness in deceitful scheming. But speaking the truth in love, we must grow up in every way into him who is the head, into Christ, from whom the whole body, joined and knit together by every ligament with which it is equipped, as each part is working properly, promotes the body's growth in building itself up in love. (Ephesians 4:11–16)

CHAPTER FIVE

A PORTRAIT OF JESUS (1:12–18)

Then I turned to see whose voice it was that spoke to me, and on turning I saw seven golden lampstands, and in the midst of the lampstands I saw one like the Son of Man, clothed with a long robe and with a golden sash across his chest. His head and his hair were white as white wool, white as snow; his eyes were like a flame of fire, his feet were like burnished bronze, refined as in a furnace, and his voice was like the sound of many waters. In his right hand he held seven stars, and from his mouth came a sharp, two-edged sword, and his face was like the sun shining with full force.

When I saw him, I fell at his feet as though dead. But he placed his right hand on me, saying, "Do not be afraid; I am the first and the last, and the living one. I was dead, and see, I am alive forever and ever; and I have the keys of Death and of Hades."

Many scholars believe that the beatitudes in Matthew's Sermon on the Mount are really meant to be a composite biography of Jesus. We very likely have a similar situation here in the Book of Revelation. We have a mosaic portrait of Jesus, with each of the elements of the composition taken from various places in the Hebrew Scriptures.

He is the Son of Man. From the prophet Ezekiel we learn that this is the designation of one who is really and truly human. From the prophet Daniel it is the title of one who is sent by God at the time of his judgment upon the world. In the Gospels it is used of Jesus in both senses. "For the Son of Man came not to be served but to serve, and to give his life a ransom for many" (Mark 10:45). "Jesus said, 'I am; and / "you will see the Son of Man / seated at the right hand of the Power," / and "coming with the clouds of heaven"'" (Mark 14:62).

Thus the members of the seven churches (lampstands) and their bishops (*angel* means *messenger of God*) can take heart for the Son of Man shares their humanity in all its frailty, (The Word was made flesh, [John 1]) and yet is the sign of the judgment of almighty God (When the Son of Man comes in his glory, [Matthew 25:31]).

He wears the robe and sash of the high priest. "He had to become like his brothers and sisters in every respect, so that he might be a merciful and faithful high priest in the service of God, to make a sacrifice of atonement for the sins of the people. Because he himself was tested by what he suffered, he is able to help those who are being tested" (Hebrews 2:17–18).

The white hair is taken from the description of the Ancient of Days (Yahweh) in Daniel 7:9. The rest of the attributes of Jesus—wisdom, power, steadfastness—are all derived from the apocalyptic visions of the Book of Daniel.

While it is not likely that any pastor is going to have such a composite portrait of Jesus made for his church, it is a verbal portrait that gave great hope to those who first heard God's word in the Book of Revelation. For us it may be unsettling in its fierceness, but it was primarily meant for communities threatened by the brutal Roman Empire at its worst. And just to make sure that we realize that Jesus is capable of triumphing over any enemy, he assures us that it is the risen Lord who speaks. He who defeated death is able to be victorious over any enemy.

For he must reign until he has put all his enemies under his feet. The last enemy to be destroyed is death. For "God has put all things in subjection under his feet." But when it says, "All things are put in subjection," it is plain that this does not include the one who put all things in subjection under him. When all things are subjected to him, then the Son himself will also be subjected to the one who put all things in subjection under him, so that God may be all in all. (1 Corinthians 15:25–28)

REFLECTION

Matthew 5:3–11 gives us another image of Jesus and his weapons for conquering:

Blessed are the poor in spirit, for theirs is the kingdom of heaven.

Blessed are those who mourn, for they will be comforted.

Blessed are the meek, for they will inherit the earth.

Blessed are those who hunger and thirst for righteousness, for they will be filled.

Blessed are the merciful, for they will receive mercy.

Blessed are the pure in heart, for they will see God.

Blessed are the peacemakers, for they will be called children of God.

Blessed are those who are persecuted for righteousness' sake, for theirs is the kingdom of heaven.

Blessed are you when people revile you and persecute you and utter all kinds of evil against you falsely on my account. Rejoice and be glad, for your reward is great in heaven, for in the same way they persecuted the prophets who were before you.

CHAPTER SIX

LETTERS TO THE CHURCHES (1:19–20)

All of a sudden the literary form changes to one that is more familiar. What the author is doing here Paul did for the churches that he had founded, sending them letters about what it means to be Christian. This is a sure sign that the author, like Paul, knows the communities and their problems and feels very comfortable in giving them advice, thus exercising a role of leadership over them.

The epistolary (letter-writing) form may seem quite alien to apocalyptic literature, and out of place here. However, they both have the same purpose. They both partake of the same prophetic task of comforting the afflicted and afflicting the comfortable. A prophet can use any literary form or symbol to challenge God's people and to recall them to their vocation: a life of holiness with himself.

With startling insight the author recognizes that a people who are persecuted can become so preoccupied with the enemy that they fail to see their own faults. They need to be reminded of the words of that great cartoon figure and theologian, Pogo. In one episode he sends word back to headquarters, "We have met the enemy, and they are us!"

It is so easy to point the finger and lay the blame for our problems at another's doorstep. And that can be a cover-up for our own spiritual blindness. The whole experience of Jesus and the early church with the Pharisees is a prime example. They were so preoccupied in pointing their fingers at the enemies of religion that they failed to notice that God's worst enemies are smug, self-righteous, religious people. Jesus put his finger on the problem of the Pharisees' spiritual blindness when he cured the man who was born physically blind. "I came into this world for judgment so that those who do not see may see, and those who do see may become blind." Some of the Pharisees nearby heard this and said to him, "Surely we are not blind, are we?" Jesus replied, "If you were blind, you would not have sin. But now that you say, 'We see,' your sin remains" (John 9:38–41).

Spiritual, like physical blindness, has many causes. One of them is making an 'idol' out of the word chosen. It is part of the job description of God's people in Exodus 19:5–6: "Now therefore, if you obey my voice and keep my covenant, you shall be my treasured possession out of all the peoples. Indeed, the whole earth is mine, but you shall be for me a priestly kingdom and a holy nation." This may be paraphrased: "If you are really serious about responding to my invitation and hold on to my love, you will be my very own, my chosen people, a community known for its holiness and a means of bringing all the world to me." God's people were to embrace the faith of Abraham and have the same effect. In Abraham's children, all the peoples of the earth were to be blessed. The Israelites were "chosen" to be a blessing on all peoples.

Unfortunately, some of them began to think that they were *chosen* because God had good taste. Too often, when reading the Bible, we presume that a word or expression found there has the same meaning as we use in common parlance today. Not so, and *chosen* is a good example. We always choose the best. We choose what has the most to offer to us. Watch someone choose a piece of fruit out of a bowl. He chooses the best. Whether it be a job, vacation, car or anything at all: We choose whatever has the most to offer to us.

God does the opposite. He chooses the least likely. "The LORD your God has chosen you out of all the peoples on earth to be his people, his treasured possession. It was not because you were more numerous than any other people that the LORD set his heart on you and chose you—for you were the fewest of all peoples. It was because the LORD loved you and kept the oath that he swore to your ancestors" (Deuteronomy 7:6–8). He chooses the poor and the powerless to do a job they are incapable of doing so that his grace may be seen through them. God chooses people not because they have something to offer him, but because he has a task for them to do.

The Israelites were God's chosen, provided they fulfilled two conditions: (1) They were to listen, i.e., be constantly alert and responsive to God's call, and (2) They were to abide in his love (covenant). When they ignored those conditions, they misunderstood the meaning of *chosen*. However, this was not a problem just for the people of old. At the end of the first century, at the same time as the Book of Revelation was being written, John, in his Gospel reminds his church: "You did not choose me but I chose you. And I appointed you to go and bear fruit, fruit that will last, so that the Father will give you whatever you ask him in my name. I am giving you these commands so that you may love one another" (John 15:16–17).

Before dealing with the complaints of the churches against the Romans, valid as they are, the author of Revelation clears the air and gets the perspective in focus by dealing with the complaints that Jesus has against them. He called them, chose them, because he has a job for them to do. Yahweh Sabaoth will take care of the Romans. The churches should look to themselves so they can continue the work of the Lord who chose them.

REFLECTION

In a world at its worst, we need a church at its best.

In a world full of sin, we need a church full of holiness.

For a world that's going down, we need a church that's going up.

For a world full of hell, we need a church full of heaven.

For a world out of tune, we need a church in harmony.

For a world full of war, we need a church full of peace.

For a world full of crime, we need a church full of honesty.

For a world full of defeat, we need a church full of victory.

For a world full of "bad news," we need a church full of "good news."

For a world ever playing, we need a church always praying.

For a discouraged world, we need an encouraging church.

(from a homily of Bishop Terry Steib, at the National Congress of Black Catholics)

CHAPTER SEVEN

EPHESUS (2:1–7)

To the angel of the church in Ephesus write: These are the words
of him who holds the seven stars in his right hand, who walks
among the seven golden lampstands:

I know your works, your toil and your patient endurance. I
know that you cannot tolerate evildoers; you have tested those
who claim to be apostles but are not, and have found them to be
false. I also know that you are enduring patiently and bearing up
for the sake of my name, and that you have not grown weary. But
I have this against you, that you have abandoned the love you had
at first. Remember then from what you have fallen; repent, and
do the works you did at first. If not, I will come to you and
remove your lampstand from its place, unless you repent. Yet this
is to your credit: you hate the works of the Nicolaitans, which I
also hate. Let anyone who has an ear listen to what the Spirit is
saying to the churches. To everyone who conquers, I will give permission to eat from the tree of life that is in the paradise of God.

The message of the Book of Revelation was meant for the universal
church, not just seven local ones. Seven is the number of fullness, or
wholeness. What the author has to say about being a Christian is not
unique to seven communities in Asia Minor.

The critique that he makes of each of these communities is meant to
help them get in shape for the challenge that is upon them. What he
praises in them are the very virtues that they need to be victors over the
enemy: "You are enduring patiently and bearing up for the sake of my
name, and that you have not grown weary" (Revelation 2:3).

But there is a problem that is going to be a very serious obstacle to
their surviving the present challenge. They have lost their first love. It is
not a question of their becoming apostates. They have not denied,

betrayed or abandoned Jesus. They simply have lost that enthusiastic love that characterized their first days of embracing him and being embraced by him. Anyone who has witnessed the excitement of a couple whose love is deep and contagious and joyful knows what he is talking about. To go back to the phrase *chosen people* is to cast light on the situation. Israel was chosen by God and embraced passionately. But, like a couple that over the years begins to take each other for granted, the chosen people's relationship with their God gradually loses its shine and tarnish hides what once was.

Contemporary slang might say that the church of Ephesus was in a rut! In a marriage this can slowly erode and dissolve what had been so vibrant. The love that they had at the beginning of their life in Christ had been so remarkable that the author remembers it. Their patient endurance, while praiseworthy, can only sustain them in surviving. And if our life with Christ is only survival, why bother?

In the Old Testament, the prophet Hosea gives us some inkling of the joy that comes when God's love is rediscovered (2:18–20):

> I will make for you a covenant on that day with the wild animals, the birds of the air, and the creeping things of the ground; and I will abolish the bow, the sword, and war from the land; and I will make you lie down in safety. And I will take you for my wife forever; I will take you for my wife in righteousness and in justice, in steadfast love, and in mercy. I will take you for my wife in faithfulness; and you shall know the LORD.

After Peter had received the Holy Spirit at Pentecost his preaching converted three thousand people. Peter had one of the worst cases of foot-in-mouth disease in the history of the church, so it certainly was not his eloquence that did it. He was so excited and enthusiastic about how much Jesus had done for him and loved him even to death on the cross that some of his hearers thought they were hearing the ravings of a drunkard. "All were amazed and perplexed, saying to one another, 'What does this mean?' But others sneered and said, 'They are filled with new wine'" (Acts 2:12–13). Peter, of course, denied that he drank before 9 A.M.!

It is exciting, joyful, exhilarating and fulfilling to be embraced by Christ. If it is not, then perhaps we have lost our first love.

"Remember then from what you have fallen; repent, and do the works you did at first. If not, I will come to you and remove your lampstand from its place, unless you repent" (Revelation 2:5).

REFLECTION

Paul's prayer for the same community at Ephesus (3:14–21) was that there should be more to our life in Christ than just surviving:

> For this reason I bow my knees before the Father, from whom every family in heaven and on earth takes its name. I pray that, according to the riches of his glory, he may grant that you may be strengthened in your inner being with power through his Spirit, and that Christ may dwell in your hearts through faith, as you are being rooted and grounded in love. I pray that you may have the power to comprehend, with all the saints, what is the breadth and length and height and depth, and to know the love of Christ that surpasses knowledge, so that you may be filled with all the fullness of God.
>
> Now to him who by the power at work within us is able to accomplish abundantly far more than all we can ask or imagine, to him be glory in the church and in Christ Jesus to all generations, forever and ever. Amen.

CHAPTER EIGHT

SMYRNA (2:8–11)

And to the angel of the church in Smyrna write: These are the words of the first and the last, who was dead and came to life:

"I know your affliction and your poverty, even though you are rich. I know the slander on the part of those who say that they are Jews and are not, but are a synagogue of Satan. Do not fear what you are about to suffer. Beware, the devil is about to throw some of you into prison so that you may be tested, and for ten days you will have affliction. Be faithful until death, and I will give you the crown of life. Let anyone who has an ear listen to what the Spirit is saying to the churches. Whoever conquers will not be harmed by the second death."

Smyrna, modern Izmir in Turkey, lies to the north of Ephesus and was in constant competition with it. This letter indicates that there was also some serious competition within the city. Perhaps it was more like sibling rivalry between two adolescent strains of Judaism: the Nazarenes (Christians) and the Jews of the Diaspora.

In the year A.D. 70, General Titus (son of Vespasian, then emperor) finished his father's work: He leveled Jerusalem and destroyed the temple. The pilgrimage feasts of the Jews from the Diaspora now made no sense. There was no sacrifice, nor a priesthood to offer it. There was a Jewish identity crisis. The Pharisees tried to solve the identity crisis by insisting that the law was the way to God. One could still be a good Jew without the temple and sacrifice.

Even before A.D. 70, Paul was able to say "been there, done that." He had been a Pharisee, and his encounter with Christ on the road to Damascus had led him to proclaim the freedom we have from the law to come to the Father through Jesus. "If anyone else has reason to be confident in the flesh, I have more: circumcised on the eighth day, a member of the people of Israel, of the tribe of Benjamin, a Hebrew born of Hebrews;

as to the law, a Pharisee; as to zeal, a persecutor of the church; as to righteousness under the law, blameless" (Philippians 3:4–6).

Paul, who was now despised by the Jews as a traitor, became suspect to many of the Christian Jews as one who was watering down the gospel. They insisted not only on clinging to the laws and practices that Jesus and his first followers had observed, but also making them part of the gospel, necessary for salvation. They infiltrated his communities and tried to get the Christians to follow their "gospel."

That occasioned his most passionate epistle, to the Galatians, called the Magna Carta of Christian freedom.

> I am astonished that you are so quickly deserting the one who called you in the grace of Christ and are turning to a different gospel—not that there is another gospel, but there are some who are confusing you and want to pervert the gospel of Christ. But even if we or an angel from heaven should proclaim to you a gospel contrary to what we proclaimed to you, let that one be accursed! As we have said before, so now I repeat, if anyone proclaims to you a gospel contrary to what you received, let that one be accursed! (Galatians 1:7–9)

> He has abolished the law with its commandments and ordinances, that he might create in himself one new humanity in place of the two, thus making peace, and might reconcile both groups to God in one body through the cross. (Ephesians 2:16)

Paul may have won the battle, but he lost the war. The church of Smyrna thirty years later was lured by the legalism that would make the law part of the gospel and co-redeemer with Jesus in salvation. "I am astonished that you are so quickly deserting the one who called you in the grace of Christ and are turning to a different gospel" (Galatians 1:6). The point is absolutely essential and Paul knew it. That is why he went head to head with Peter over it (Galatians 2:11–14).

It has been said that this passage about the false Jews and the synagogue of Satan are indications of the anti-Semitism that has been and is supposedly inherent in Christianity. That is not at all true. Neither here nor other places in the New Testament are the Jewish people condemned. Every suspect passage, if understood in its historical context is seen to be the intemperate and emotional outburst of two rival siblings, Jews who were Pharisees and Jews who were Nazarenes. After the destruction of the temple, they competed for converts to their "Way." Even today in Israel, the followers of one rabbi will accuse the followers of another of being false Jews in language that is unprintable. That's exactly what was going on in New Testament times. It can hardly be labeled anti-Semitism.

There is no denying, however, that Christians have misunderstood the words of the New Testament to support their prejudice. Such anti-Semitism is a serious sin, so much so that Pope John Paul II apologized for it at the Western Wall in Jerusalem. At the same time there are bound to be differences between two people, both of whom claim to be the true Israel.

> May I never boast of anything except the cross of our Lord Jesus Christ, by which the world has been crucified to me, and I to the world. For neither circumcision nor uncircumcision is anything; but a new creation is everything! As for those who will follow this rule—peace be upon them, and mercy, and upon the Israel of God. (Galatians 6:14–16)

REFLECTION

> I urge you…that you may instruct certain people not to teach any different doctrine, and not to occupy themselves with myths…that promote speculations rather than the divine training that is known by faith. But the aim of such instruction is love that comes from a pure heart, a good conscience, and sincere faith. Some people have deviated from these and turned to meaningless talk, desiring to be teachers of the law, without understanding either what they are saying or the things about which they make assertions.
>
> Now we know that the law is good, if one uses it legitimately. This means understanding that the law is laid down not for the

innocent but for the lawless and disobedient, for the godless and sinful, for the unholy and profane, for those who kill their father or mother, for murderers, fornicators, sodomites, slave traders, liars, perjurers, and whatever else is contrary to the sound teaching that conforms to the glorious gospel of the blessed God, which he entrusted to me. (1 Timothy 1:3–11)

CHAPTER NINE

PERGAMUM (2:12–17)

And to the angel of the church in Pergamum write: These are the words of him who has the sharp two-edged sword:

"I know where you are living, where Satan's throne is. Yet you are holding fast to my name, and you did not deny your faith in me even in the days of Antipas my witness, my faithful one, who was killed among you, where Satan lives. But I have a few things against you: you have some there who hold to the teaching of Balaam, who taught Balak to put a stumbling block before the people of Israel, so that they would eat food sacrificed to idols and practice fornication. So you also have some who hold to the teaching of the Nicolaitans. Repent then. If not, I will come to you soon and make war against them with the sword of my mouth. Let anyone who has an ear listen to what the Spirit is saying to the churches. To everyone who conquers I will give some of the hidden manna, and I will give a white stone, and on the white stone is written a new name that no one knows except the one who receives it."

This is the second time that the Nicolaitans appear (also at Ephesus) and it is not at all clear exactly what their problem was. Looking at the context and reading between the lines, however, it seems that they were believers in compromise. They are just the opposite of Antipas, who witnessed to the lordship of Jesus by the shedding of his blood.

The crisis in Pergamum had to do with the claims of the emperor to the political and religious loyalty of his subjects. He was lord and reigned from his throne (Satan's throne!). Every Roman subject had to acknowledge this publicly and accept a sign of compliance.

"Those who worship the beast and its image, will receive a mark on their foreheads or on their hands, they will also drink the wine of God's wrath.... There is no rest day or night for those who worship the beast and its image and for anyone who receives the mark of its name" (Revelation 14:9–11).

A dilemma is defined as two facts in conflict. This was a dilemma of life threatening proportions. Should Antipas be their model? Or was there another way out, apparently proposed by "Nicolaus"? The reasoning of the Nicolaitans would run something like this: It is only a pinch of incense cast on the coals. We can make an external gesture of loyalty before the statue of the emperor but know in our hearts where our real loyalty lies. One doesn't have to be a religious fanatic, the Nicolaitians would reason. All others in town who had their own gods did not feel that they were abandoning them when they offered a gesture of loyalty to the emperor. Why should the Christians be so rigid about it? After all, it was simply adapting the gospel to an extremely complex political situation.

Loyalty to the Roman Empire and its leaders was a Christian virtue Paul had proclaimed about thirty years before:

> Let every person be subject to the governing authorities; for there is no authority except from God, and those authorities that exist have been instituted by God. Therefore whoever resists authority resists what God has appointed, and those who resist will incur judgment. For rulers are not a terror to good conduct, but to bad. Do you wish to have no fear of the authority? Then do what is good, and you will receive its approval; for it is God's servant for your good. (Romans 13:1–4)

But times had changed. Emperor worship had not yet taken hold and been identified with civil loyalty to the Roman Empire when Paul wrote. The two diverse attitudes toward the Empire, Romans and Revelation, indicate how alert the church must be. The state that is praised at one time may need to be condemned at another time. Paul knew that the gospel could sink its roots in any culture, but the author of Revelation knew that one must be wary of compromising the gospel by values that are alien to it. Such compromise can destroy the gospel. The Nicolaitans' seemingly innocuous and trifling compromise would have struck at the heart of Christianity, for only Jesus is Lord.

A case closer to our own times illustrates the point. At the end of the Second World War, those accused of collaboration with the Nazi occupiers of their nation claimed that their heart was not in it. They claimed to be loyal citizens who went through the externals of cooperation. Such schizophrenia was seen as treachery, and the traitors were condemned.

REFLECTION

For where your treasure is, there your heart will be also. (Matthew 6:21)

No one can serve two masters; for a slave will either hate the one and love the other, or be devoted to the one and despise the other. You cannot serve God and wealth. (6:24)

Therefore I want you to understand...no one can say "Jesus is Lord" except by the Holy Spirit. (1 Corinthians 12:3)

CHAPTER TEN

THYATIRA (2:18–29)

And to the angel of the church in Thyatira write: These are the words of the Son of God, who has eyes like a flame of fire, and whose feet are like burnished bronze:

"I know your works—your love, faith, service, and patient endurance. I know that your last works are greater than the first. But I have this against you: you tolerate that woman Jezebel, who calls herself a prophet and is teaching and beguiling my servants to practice fornication and to eat food sacrificed to idols. I gave her time to repent, but she refuses to repent of her fornication. Beware, I am throwing her on a bed, and those who commit adultery with her I am throwing into great distress, unless they repent of her doings; and I will strike her children dead. And all the churches will know that I am the one who searches minds and hearts, and I will give to each of you as your works deserve. But to the rest of you in Thyatira, who do not hold this teaching, who have not learned what some call 'the deep things of Satan,' to you I say, I do not lay on you any other burden; only hold fast to what you have until I come. To everyone who conquers and continues to do my works to the end,

I will give authority over the nations;
to rule them with an iron rod,
as when clay pots are shattered—

even as I also received authority from my Father. To the one who conquers I will also give the morning star. Let anyone who has an ear listen to what the Spirit is saying to the churches."

Many people presume that the divisions in the church started in 1517 with the Protestant Reformation. Those with a little more knowledge of history will also recall the split (schism) between East and West, Rome and Constantinople in 1053.

The New Testament, however, is a witness to the fragmentation that began shortly after the Resurrection. In no time the Apostles had to call the Council of Jerusalem to attempt to reconcile the factions that arose over the observance of Judaism (Acts 15:1–41). In Corinth, Paul encountered a personality cult that divided the church. "So let no one boast about human leaders. For all things are yours, whether Paul or Apollos or Cephas or the world or life or death or the present or the future—all belong to you, and you belong to Christ, and Christ belongs to God" (1 Corinthians 3:21–23). Behind the letters of John is the problem of the heretics who split (the Greek word is *schism*) from the community, denying the humanity of Christ (Docetism).

Thyatira seems to have generated a double-pronged heresy that involved sex and sacrifice. The author goes back and uses the story of Jezebel, wife of King Ahab of Israel. From her homeland of Sidon (modern Lebanon), she brought her chaplains of the cult of Baal and Ashtarte, the divine couple who were in charge of fertility. King Ahab of Israel built a temple for them in his capital. Their cult involved the use of temple prostitutes having sex (the act of fertility) with those seeking fertility for their family, flocks and lands. This liturgy naturally proved attractive to some people who suddenly became very religious! The Prophet Elijah was enraged and called for a contest between himself and the prophets of Baal, between the creator of the world and the so-called god and goddess of fertility (1 Kings 16–19).

We don't know exactly what was going on in Thyatira along those lines, but it was certainly an aberration of the gospel. This is not the first time that the gift of sex was abused in the name of religion. In Corinth, Paul was informed that one of his Christian converts was proclaiming that one's sexual activity had nothing to do with life in Christ: He was only doing what comes naturally. Paul's challenge? You wouldn't be acting that way if you knew who you were:

> The body is meant not for fornication but for the Lord, and the Lord for the body. And God raised the Lord and will also raise us by his power. Do you not know that your bodies are members of

Christ? Should I therefore take the members of Christ and make them members of a prostitute? ...Or do you not know that your body is a temple of the Holy Spirit within you, which you have from God, and that you are not your own? For you were bought with a price; therefore glorify God in your body. (1 Corinthians 6:13–20)

The second prong of the sectarianism in Thyatira was also a problem in Corinth: May a Christian eat meat that has been offered to idols? More fundamentally, must a Christian be a vegetarian, since all the meat was first sacrificed and the pagan temples were the butcher shops? This author condemns eating such meat. It would send the wrong signals, making it appear that Christians could be as eclectic in religion as their pagan neighbors. That would be an attack on the Lord Jesus, who is the Way, the Truth and the Life with no competitors.

Paul, also in the name of the gospel, has a more nuanced view. "Now concerning food sacrificed to idols: "...all things are lawful," but not all things are beneficial. "All things are lawful," but not all things build up. Do not seek your own advantage, but that of the other. Eat whatever is sold in the meat market without raising any question on the ground of conscience, for

the earth and its fullness are the Lord's.... Therefore, my dear friends, flee from the worship of idols. I speak as to sensible people; judge, for yourselves what I say. The cup of blessing that we bless, is it not a sharing in the blood of Christ? The bread that we break, is it not a sharing in the body of Christ? Because there is one bread, we who are many are one body, for we all partake of the one bread. Consider the people of Israel are not those who eat the sacrifices partners in the altar?... What do I imply then? That food sacrificed to idols is anything, or that an idol is anything? So, whether you eat or drink, or whatever you do, do everything for the glory of God. Give no offense to Jews or to Greeks or to the church of God, just as I try to please everyone in everything I do, not seeking my own advantage, but that of many, so that they may be saved. Be imitators of me, as I am of Christ. (1 Corinthians 8:1; 10:14–33; 11:1)

Apparently the church has enough room even for those who have different opinions on something as important as meat offered to idols.

REFLECTION

Change and adaptation are intrinsic to the pilgrim church. That is why we have four Gospels and not just one. Each Evangelist had to adapt it when evangelizing his own church.

> The individual churches, intimately built up, not only of people, but also of aspirations, of riches and limitations, of ways of praying and loving, of looking at life and the world which distinguishes this or that human gathering have the task of assimilating the essence of the Gospel message and transposing it, without the slightest betrayal of its essential truth, into the language that these particular people understand, then of proclaiming it in this language.
>
> The transposition has to be done with the discernment, seriousness, respect and competence which the matter calls for in the field of liturgical expression and in the areas of catechesis, theological formulation, secondary ecclesiastical structures and ministries. And the word "language" here should be understood less in the semantic or literary sense than in the sense that one would call anthropological or cultural.
>
> The question is undoubtedly a delicate one. Evangelization loses much of its force and effectiveness if it does not take into consideration the actual people to whom it is addressed, if it does not use their language, their signs and symbols, if it does not answer the questions they are asking, if it does not have an impact on their concrete life. But on the other hand, Evangelization risks losing its power and disappearing altogether if one empties or adulterates its content under the pretext of transplanting it; if in

other words one sacrifices this reality and destroys the unity without which there is no universality, out of a wish to adapt a universal reality to a local situation. Only a church which preserves the awareness of her universality and shows that she is in fact universal is capable of having a message which can be heard by all, regardless of regional frontiers. (Paul VI, "On Evangelization," 1964)

CHAPTER ELEVEN

SARDIS (3:1–6)

And to the angel of the church in Sardis write: These are the words of him who has the seven spirits of God and the seven stars:

"I know your works; you have a name of being alive, but you are dead. Wake up, and strengthen what remains and is on the point of death, for I have not found your works perfect in the sight of my God. Remember then what you received and heard; obey it, and repent. If you do not wake up, I will come like a thief, and you will not know at what hour I will come to you. Yet you have still a few persons in Sardis who have not soiled their clothes; they will walk with me, dressed in white, for they are worthy. If you conquer, you will be clothed like them in white robes, and I will not blot your name out of the book of life; I will confess your name before my Father and before his angels. Let anyone who has an ear listen to what the Spirit is saying to the churches."

Poor Sardis is chastised severely for being dead. Presumably the church there knows what its problem is. But we haven't a clue. Whatever it is, it has been allowed to happen because they have a poor memory. They have forgotten. They are not accused of harboring heretics or consorting with those who would water down the gospel. Their sin is that they have forgotten; they are in a spiritual coma.

But they have company in their misery. Paul warns some in the nearby city of Ephesus:

Sleeper, awake!
　　Rise from the dead,
and Christ will shine on you. (Ephesians 5:14)

Even though the exact problem that has placed Sardis in such an unenviable position with its Lord is unclear, there are some clues to its malady.

"Remember then what you have seen and heard; obey it and repent."

Like all the churches that are criticized in these letters, they have been guilty of idolatry, although the specific form and shape of the idol is not revealed to us. They are called to repent. To repent comes from the Greek word *metanoia,* a change of mind or of attitude. They are to get their priorities straight and do an about-face. They must name the idol that has turned them away from the gospel, from Jesus whom they have seen and heard.

Those who seriously read the Bible can easily misconceive what idol worship is all about. Very often when we read about it in the condemnations of the prophets we visualize a concrete, tangible figure made by humans out of wood or metal. But we should not underestimate our ancestors. They may have been less sophisticated, but they were not naïve. Just as a statue of Christ, the Virgin or one of the saints carried in procession today is a sign of heavenly advocacy and protection, so were the idols of our ancestors. They did not replace Yahweh. There was room for him, but he did not have the whole field. Indeed, as far as transportation out of Egypt was concerned, he had no rival. But in an age of specialization, they did not want to put all of their eggs in one basket. Their neighbors claimed that there were other powers (gods) whose specialty was fertility, prosperity, war, future security or sex. They, not the statues symbolizing them, were the real idols. An idol is anything that his people put in the place of Yahweh. Isaiah is right on target:

> O house of Jacob,
>> come, let us walk
>> in the light of the LORD!
> For you have forsaken the ways of your people,
>> O house of Jacob.
> Indeed they are full of diviners from the east
>> and of soothsayers like the Philistines,
>> and they clasp hands with foreigners.
> Their land is filled with silver and gold,
>> and there is no end to their treasures;
> their land is filled with horses,

and there is no end to their chariots.
Their land is filled with idols;
> they bow down to the work of their hands,
to what their own fingers have made. (Isaiah 2:5–8)

Diviners (what does the future hold?), soothsayers (what decision should I make?), clasping hands with foreigners (seeking protection?), silver and gold (bank accounts?), treasures (insider trading?), horses and chariots (military industrial complex?): All of these are idols, whether or not they are symbolized by a figure in wood, bronze or gold, are "what their (our) fingers have made."

Is Isaiah's advice to Jerusalem any different from Jesus' admonition to Sardis? "Turn back to him whom you have deeply betrayed, O people of Israel. For on that day all of you shall throw away your idols of silver and idols of gold, which your hands have sinfully made for you" (Isaiah 31:6).

REFLECTION

In the early community, both Matthew's Gospel and the epistles of Paul bear witness to segments of the community who were unwilling to let go of the past. They wanted to hold on to the institutions of Judaism. Paul had to smash that idol:

> Yet whatever gains I had, these I have come to regard as loss because of Christ. More than that, I regard everything as loss because of the surpassing value of knowing Christ Jesus my Lord. For his sake I have suffered the loss of all things, and I regard them as rubbish, in order that I may gain Christ and be found in him, not having a righteousness of my own that comes from the law, but one that comes through faith in Christ, the righteousness from God based on faith. I want to know Christ and the power of his resurrection and the sharing of his sufferings by becoming like him in his death, if somehow I may attain the resurrection from the dead. (Philippians 3:7–11)

Saint Benedict said the same thing more succinctly: "Let nothing be preferred to Christ!"

CHAPTER TWELVE

PHILADELPHIA (3:7–13)

And to the angel of the church in Philadelphia write:
> These are the words of the holy one
>> the true one,
> who has the key of David,
> who opens and no one will shut,
> who shuts and no one opens:

"I know your works. Look, I have set before you an open door, which no one is able to shut. I know that you have but little power, and yet you have kept my word and have not denied my name. I will make those of the synagogue of Satan who say that they are Jews and are not, but are lying—I will make them come and bow down before your feet, and they will learn that I have loved you. Because you have kept my word of patient endurance, I will keep you from the hour of trial that is coming on the whole world to test the inhabitants of the earth. I am coming soon; hold fast to what you have, so that no one may seize your crown. If you conquer, I will make you a pillar in the temple of my God; you will never go out of it. I will write on you the name of my God, and the name of the city of my God, the new Jerusalem that comes down from my God out of heaven, and my own new name. Let anyone who has an ear listen to what the Spirit is saying to the churches."

From our twenty-first century perspective of ecumenism, the criticism in this letter of the synagogue of Satan and the pseudo-Jews may seem insulting. It is inconceivable for us to imagine Jews, even some converted to Christianity, trying to proselytize us to live their way of life. Religious freedom demands that we respect each other.

Vatican II said of religious freedom:

> The Church is being faithful to the truth of the gospel and is following the way of Christ and the apostles when she recognizes, and gives support to, the principle of religious freedom as befitting the dignity of man and as being in accord with divine revelation. Throughout the ages the church has kept safe and handed on the doctrine received from the Master and from the apostles. In the life of the People of God as it has made its pilgrim way through the vicissitudes of human history, there have at times appeared ways of acting which were less in accord with the spirit of the gospel and even opposed to it. (*Dignitatis Humanae*, 12)

But history is repeating itself in Israel today, where groups of Jews are excommunicating each other over interpretations of the Torah. What happened in ancient Philadelphia is happening today. It is not a question merely of legal interpretation; nor is it a question of Torah observance. It is a question of identity.

In Israel today, where the right-leaning Orthodox have the upper hand, the question of who is a Jew is paramount. Rabbis of Reform, Conservative and other groups cannot perform official religious functions such as marriages, because they are not considered authentic Jews, even though born of a Jewish mother. When one group is in a position to define who is an authentic Jew, a real member of God's people, excluding all who do not worship and behave as they do, then those excluded have an identity crisis—as do the excluders!

For the author writing to the Christians of Philadelphia, to be coerced into embracing the law as a necessary component of salvation is a direct attack on the role of Christ. It puts excess baggage on the "gospel." It is in Christ that we have our identity, not in the law. At the time of writing, the Christians had recently been expelled from the synagogue and are in the throes of an identity crisis. Some years before, Paul pointed toward the solution to the problem:

> We ourselves are Jews by birth and not Gentile sinners; yet we know that a person is justified not by the works of the law but

through faith in Jesus Christ. And we have come to believe in Christ Jesus, so that we might be justified by faith in Christ, and not by doing the works of the law, because no one will be justified by the works of the law. But if, in our effort to be justified in Christ, we ourselves have been found to be sinners, is Christ then a servant of sin? Certainly not! But if I build up again the very things that I once tore down, then I demonstrate that I am a transgressor. For through the law I died to the law, so that I might live to God. I have been crucified with Christ; and it is no longer I who live, but it is Christ who lives in me. And the life I now live in the flesh I live by faith in the Son of God, who loved me and gave himself for me. I do not nullify the grace of God; for if justification comes through the law, then Christ died for nothing. (Galatians 2:15–21)

REFLECTION

Christ, as a Light, Illumine and Guide Me.
Christ as a Shield, O'ershadow and Cover Me.
Christ Be Under, Me Christ Be Over Me, Christ Be Before Me, Behind Me, About Me.
Christ This Day, Be Within and Without Me
Christ the Lowly and the Meek,
Christ the All-Powerful, Be in the Heart of Each to Whom I
Speak
In the Mouth of Each Who Speaks to Me,
In All Who Draw Near Me or See Me or Hear Me.
(Prayer of Saint Patrick)

CHAPTER THIRTEEN

LAODICEA (3:14–22)

And to the angel of the church in Laodicea write: The words of the Amen, the faithful and true witness, the origin of God's creation:

"I know your works; you are neither cold nor hot. I wish that you were either cold or hot. So, because you are lukewarm, and neither cold nor hot, I am about to spit you out of my mouth. For you say, "I am rich, I have prospered, and I need nothing." You do not realize that you are wretched, pitiable, poor, blind, and naked. Therefore I counsel you to buy from me gold refined by fire so that you may be rich; and white robes to clothe you and to keep the shame of your nakedness from being seen; and salve to anoint your eyes so that you may see. I reprove and discipline those whom I love. Be earnest, therefore, and repent. Listen! I am standing at the door, knocking; if you hear my voice and open the door, I will come in to you and eat with you, and you with me. To the one who conquers I will give a place with me on my throne, just as I myself conquered and sat down with my Father on his throne. Let anyone who has an ear listen to what the Spirit is saying to the churches."

At the end of Paul's letter to the Colossians, he mentions a letter to the Laodiceans and that there should be a mutual sharing of the letters that he wrote to each community. Perhaps one day, when archaeologists have done their work, we shall hear proclaimed from the pulpit: "A reading from the letter of Saint Paul to the Laodiceans." It tempts the strain of curiosity in each of us, but, if God thought it was necessary for us to have it, we would have it. We do not, and will have to be satisfied with Revelation's letter to that church.

The churches of Revelation are battered by enemies: the Roman Empire trying to take the place of God, the Nicolaitans who would counsel compromise with its blasphemous demands, the Jews and the Judaizers who would lead them away from the gospel to the comfortable "good old days" of the law, and the enticingly attractive tenets of Jezebel who would turn the liturgy into an orgy.

But seven is the number of fullness, and this is the seventh letter. It is the summit of the condemnations, not of a tangible enemy but of the unseen cancer within. The criticism is startling and nauseating. "You make me throw up. Thinking of you makes me vomit. You make me sick to my stomach. I spit you out into the gutter." No matter how you translate it, it is disgusting. What could cause such a reaction?

Nothing. They were guilty of nothing. Their faith was *pro forma*. They accepted the gospel but they did not embrace it. As far as material success was concerned, they could not be faulted. They were prosperous. As far as the gospel was concerned they had slid down the soapy chute of smug and comfortable mediocrity.

They didn't stick out from the crowd of pagans around them. No one would even notice that they were Christian. There was no passion for the gospel, no enthusiasm or excitement. Church was just one more club that they were members of. And the lukewarmness of their Christian faith would not set anyone on fire.

In his decree on evangelization, Paul VI described what it means to be a Christian:

Take a Christian or a handful of Christians who in the midst of their own community, show their capacity for understanding and acceptance, their sharing of life and destiny with other people, their solidarity with the efforts of all for whatever is noble and good. Let us suppose that in addition, they radiate in an altogether simple and unaffected way their faith in values that go beyond present values, and their hope in something that is not seen and that one would not dare to imagine. Through this wordless witness these Christians stir up irresistible questions in the hearts of those who see how they live: Why are they like this? Why do they live in this way? What or who is it that inspires them? Why are they in our midst?

That's not the Laodiceans. They didn't raise questions in anyone's hearts. German theologian Karl Rahner wrote of "Anonymous Christians." The Laodiceans were innocuous Christians. The only effect their faith had was to cause Jesus to vomit. They were "wretched, pitiable, poor, blind, and naked" (Revelation 3:17) and didn't even know it. Their material success had made them unaware of what failures they were in Jesus' eyes.

Did they wake up and come alive when they read this indictment? Jesus didn't give up on them. He was knocking at their door, but it was up to them to open it.

REFLECTION

Wisdom seen on a banner:
"If You Were Brought to Trial for Being a Christian,
Would There Be Enough Evidence to Convict You?"

CHAPTER FOURTEEN

HEAVENLY LITURGY (4:1–11)

After this I looked, and there in heaven a door stood open! And the first voice, which I had heard speaking to me like a trumpet, said, "Come up here, and I will show you what must take place after this." At once I was in the spirit, and there in heaven stood a throne, with one seated on the throne! And the one seated there looks like jasper and carnelian, and around the throne is a rainbow that looks like an emerald. Around the throne are twenty-four thrones, and seated on the thrones are twenty-four elders, dressed in white robes, with golden crowns on their heads. Coming from the throne are flashes of lightning, and rumblings and peals of thunder, and in front of the throne burn seven flaming torches, which are the seven spirits of God; and in front of the throne there is something like a sea of glass, like crystal.

Around the throne, and on each side of the throne, are four living creatures, full of eyes in front and behind: the first living creature like a lion, the second living creature like an ox, the third living creature with a face like a human face, and the fourth living creature like a flying eagle. And the four living creatures, each of them with six wings, are full of eyes all around and inside. Day and night without ceasing they sing,

"Holy, holy, holy,
the Lord God the Almighty,
who was and is and is to come."

And whenever the living creatures give glory and honor and thanks to the one who is seated on the throne, who lives forever and ever, the twenty-four elders fall before the one who is seated on the throne and worship the one who lives forever and ever; they cast their crowns before the throne, singing,

"You are worthy, our Lord and God,
    to receive glory and honor and power,
  for you created all things,
      and by your will they existed and were created."

To understand this chapter, the language it uses and the context in which it was first read are important.

Mythical symbolism, using the Greek language but heavily influenced by Aramaic grammar, is the vehicle through which the author conveys God's message. And that was done nineteen hundred years ago. Is it any wonder that we have to work a bit to get at the truth? And truth there is. Myth in the biblical sense does not mean fairy tale. It does not imply that there is only fantasy or entertainment, and no truth.

Myth is our attempt to express the inexpressible, to put into words what words cannot contain, to convey the deepest mysteries of life through words that are inadequate. We use mythical language all of the time. A husband calls his wife "honey." She calls him "tiger." They refer to their daughter as "princess." She says that a new dress is "to die for." He says that his stockbroker is a "wizard," and his new car is "dynamite" or a "lemon." They all agree that the ice cream is "heavenly," and that a sick friend is going through "hell." I am writing this in Jamaica, where someone trying to board a crowded bus yells: "Small yo'self, mon!" There is truth in every affirmation, but a foreigner trying to learn the English language could only be confused.

A further complication is that one reality may have multiple symbols in the mind of the author. Jesus is the Pantocrator, the Amen, the Lamb (as well as the shepherd!) and the lion of the tribe of Judah. On the other hand one image may refer to a multiplicity of realities. The woman of chapter twelve may be Mary, the mother of Jesus, the virgin daughter Israel, the mother of the church or all of the above.

And we are foreigners to the world of the Book of Revelation and to the heavenly realities that the author now tries to convey. If we work at it we may be able to perceive the truth conveyed by some of his language. But it should be no surprise if the deepest meaning of some of his mythical language still evades us. We will try to demythologize and put the eternal truths in modern language. It may still be mythical language, but it is our own, a language that expresses the same ancient truth for our day.

In chapter four there is a leap from earth to heaven, from the pilgrim church to the "church triumphant." If the deep mysteries of life on earth that are part of our experience are difficult to encapsulate in our feeble language, no language on earth can capture the joy and ecstasy of heaven by one who was having a mystical experience "in the spirit."

Up until now, all has been prologue and preview of coming attractions. Now the apocalypse begins. It commences however, not on earth where the problem is, but in heaven, where the solution is.

We are brought into a liturgical assembly. Some of the symbols defy the imagination: "one who looks like jasper and carnelian" surrounded by a "rainbow that looks like an emerald." Don't even try to visualize it. Just allow yourself to get caught up into what is indescribable. The author is not trying to paint a picture, but to draw us into the aura of a great mystery.

Twenty-four elders bring together in the heavenly court, the twelve patriarchs of the Old Testament, and the twelve prophets of the New Testament. Everybody who is anybody is there, including representatives of every level of creation—lion, ox, eagle and human. They are borrowed from the symbols in the visions of the prophet Ezekiel, and eventually were given a new meaning by the church who used them to symbolize the four Evangelists. They are full of eyes, because unlike their fellow creatures on earth they can see what is really going on. In the language of today's financial world, they are participating in insider trading.

All are involved in worship, which means that we are being given a glimpse into the heavenly liturgy. The "Holy, Holy, Holy" which Isaiah heard the seraphim singing in his vision of the heavenly liturgy (Isaiah 6) is still being chanted by the participants of the eternal liturgy. And since the purpose of all liturgy is to give ourselves to God who gives himself to us, our representatives from both the Old and New Testament relinquish the signs of their power, their crowns. And the sea, which is the symbol of chaos and is the realm of anti-God forces (cf. Revelation 13:1) in the

Hebrew Scriptures, is calm and as smooth as glass in the presence of its maker.

Then the Lord God is praised for his masterpiece of creation, which came to be by his willing it. Thus the author strikes a blow at any dualistic Manichaeism. Creation is good, not the realm of the powers of darkness. It is God's gift. It is not evil, even though people can be.

REFLECTION

Holy, Holy, Holy!
Lord God Almighty,
Early in the morning our song shall rise to thee.
Holy, holy, holy, merciful and mighty!
God in three persons, Blessed Trinity.
Holy, holy, holy!
All the saints adore thee,
Casting down their golden crowns around the glassy sea;
Cherubim and Seraphim falling down before thee;
Which wert and art and ever more shall be.
Holy, holy, holy,
Though the darkness hide thee,
Though the eye made blind by sin thy glory may not see,
Only thou art holy,
there is none beside thee,
Perfect in power, in love and purity.
(Reginald Heber)

CHAPTER FIFTEEN

HEAVENLY LITURGY CONTINUED (4:1–11)

Now we must try to put ourselves in the position of those who first heard this letter. The author intended that it be proclaimed when the community was gathered. "Blessed is the one who reads aloud the words of the prophecy, and blessed are those who hear and who keep what is written in it" (1:3). The community is at worship for the "breaking of the bread." The word has spread that there is a message from the penal colony at Patmos. The one presiding, "the Angel of the church," reads the introduction and greeting. Then there is the penitential rite with the call to conversion in chapters two and three.

Then chapter four begins the description of the glorious heavenly liturgy with its triumphant choral pieces, "Holy, holy, holy" and "You are worthy, our Lord and God, to receive glory and honor and power." The Christians are huddled together, fearful of making a sound that would attract the attention of the authorities. A knock at the door would send them running for cover.

At the description of the heavenly liturgy, they are filled with hope. They are not alone. What they are doing on earth is the same as what is going on in heaven. Their little hovel is united with the celestial realms. In the liturgy, heaven and earth are united.

The Second Vatican Council proclaimed:

In the earthly liturgy, by way of foretaste, we share in that heavenly liturgy which is celebrated in the holy city of Jerusalem, toward which we journey as pilgrims, and in which Christ is sitting at the right hand of God, a minister of the sanctuary and of the true tabernacle; we sing a hymn to the Lord's glory with all the warriors of the heavenly army; venerating the memory of the saints, we hope for some part and fellowship with them; we eagerly await the Saviour, our Lord Jesus Christ, until He, our life, shall appear and we too, shall appear with him in glory. (*Constitution on the Sacred Liturgy,* 8)

The *Constitution on the Sacred Liturgy* then refers to Philippians 3:20:

Our citizenship is in heaven, and it is from there that we are expecting a Savior, the Lord Jesus Christ. He will transform the body of our humiliation that it may be conformed to the body of his glory, by the power that also enables him to make all things subject to himself. Therefore, my brothers and sisters, whom I love and long for, my joy and crown, stand firm in the Lord in this way, my beloved.

and Colossians 3:4:

So if you have been raised with Christ, seek the things that are above, where Christ is, seated at the right hand of God. Set your minds on things that are above, not on things that are on earth, for you have died, and your life is hidden with Christ in God. When Christ who is your life is revealed, then you also will be revealed with him in glory.

Since the heavenly liturgy can be nothing less than the sacrifice of Christ, this may be confusing. Was not his sacrifice completed with his death on Calvary? How can it now be continuing in heaven?

Recent biblical scholarship, especially that by Pere Roland deVaux, O.P., of the Ecole Biblique in Jerusalem *(Sacrifice in the Old Testament)* has shown that the essence of sacrifice was never in the death or destruction of the victim. It was in the transformation of the victim. Sacrifice was a sign. The one offering a lamb was saying to God that he was offering the lamb in place of himself. As the lamb would be changed and transformed, so would the offerer be transformed in union with God. God does not like dead lambs, he likes live people. The lamb is sacrificed to remind the one offering it that he must offer himself in transformation.

If the transformation does not occur, then the sacrifice is a lie, and the one offering is a hypocrite. God does not tolerate such duplicity. The prophets put their finger right on it: "Whoever slaughters an ox is like one who kills a human being; whoever sacrifices a lamb, like one who breaks a dog's neck" (Isaiah 66:3). If the transformation of the one offering does not happen it is not sacrifice; it's the butchering of an animal.

Since the very meaning of sacrifice is in the transformation of the victim, then the sacrifice of Christ is not over and done with in his death.

He is transformed in Resurrection, in which he passes from time into eternity. Thus his sacrifice becomes eternal. It is still going on. It is more proper to say that Jesus is sacrificing than that he sacrificed.

This helps to make sense of what used to be rather an enigmatic part of the first Eucharistic Prayer: "Almighty God, we pray that your angel may take this sacrifice to your altar in heaven. Then as we receive from this altar the sacred body and blood of your Son, let us be filled with every heavenly grace and blessing." The earthly liturgy, the Mass, is a sacrifice not because it makes the past present but because it brings eternity into time. The eternal sacrifice of Christ is made present on our alter each time we "do this in memory" of Jesus.

The Christians of Asia Minor were given great hope by the author who reminded them that in the liturgy they were lifted out of the chaos of the world around them into the eternal sacrifice of their Lord who was not defeated, even by death.

REFLECTION

Father, all-powerful and ever-living God,
We do well always and everywhere to give you thanks
Through Jesus Christ, Our Lord.
We praise you with greater joy than ever in this Easter season,
When Christ became our paschal sacrifice.
He is still our priest,
Our advocate who always pleads our cause.
Christ is the victim who dies no more,
The Lamb once slain who lives forever.
The joy of the resurrection renews the whole world,
While the choirs of heaven sing forever to your glory.

Holy, holy, holy, Lord God of power and might,
Heaven and earth are full of your glory,
Hosanna in the highest.
Blessed is he who comes in the name of the Lord.
Hosanna in the highest.
(Preface of Easter III)

CHAPTER SIXTEEN

THE LITURGY OF THE WORD (5:1–14)

Then I saw in the right hand of the one seated on the throne a scroll written on the inside and on the back, sealed with seven seals; and I saw a mighty angel proclaiming with a loud voice, "Who is worthy to open the scroll and break its seals?" And no one in heaven or on earth or under the earth was able to open the scroll or to look into it. And I began to weep bitterly because no one was found worthy to open the scroll or to look into it. Then one of the elders said to me, "Do not weep. See, the Lion of the tribe of Judah, the Root of David, has conquered, so that he can open the scroll and its seven seals.

Then I saw between the throne and the four living creatures and among the elders a Lamb standing as if it had been slaughtered, having seven horns and seven eyes, which are the seven spirits of God sent out into all the earth. He went and took the scroll from the right hand of the one who was seated on the throne. When he had taken the scroll, the four living creatures and the twenty-four elders fell before the Lamb, each holding a harp and golden bowls full of incense, which are the prayers of the saints. They sing a new song:

"You are worthy to take the scroll
 and to open its seals,
for you were slaughtered and by your blood you ransomed
  for God
  saints from every tribe and language and people and
   nation;
you have made them to be a kingdom and priests serving
  our God,
  and they will reign on earth."

Then I looked, and I heard the voice of many angels surrounding the throne and the living creatures and the elders; they numbered myriads of myriads and thousands of thousands, singing with full voice,

> "Worthy is the Lamb that was slaughtered
> to receive power and wealth and wisdom and might
> and honor and glory and blessing!"

Then I heard every creature in heaven and on earth and under the earth and in the sea, and all that is in them, singing,

> "To the one seated on the throne and to the Lamb
> be blessing and honor and glory and might
> forever and ever!"

And the four living creatures said, "Amen!" And the elders fell down and worshiped.

The liturgy continues with the celebration of the Word. It is on a scroll which God wrote on both sides. As I sit at my laptop writing this, I try to imagine God doing the same thing. It is nothing new to say that God spoke. However, to say that he wrote on both sides of a piece of sheepskin (to save money?) requires a vivid imagination. But then when the author says that the lamb took the scroll, it defies the imagination. How does a lamb take hold of a scroll? And how did he feel about the writing material that was the skin of one of his kinfolk? I suspect that the author expected to evoke a smile before things get too serious. Either that or he has forgotten that every image, every analogy is limited. Every figure of speech falls short of the truth it is trying to convey as Paul found out with the potter and his clay. To complicate matters we speak of "mixed metaphors," like that of the woman who complained of her neighbor who "stabbed me in the back, right to my face."

Any good liturgy includes a choir. But anything worth doing is worth overdoing! We are told in 4:8 that the four living creatures form a quartet. Not to be outdone, the twenty-four senior citizens form a chorus. Then thousands and thousands of angels join in the praise (5:11). And for the grand finale *"every creature in heaven and on earth and under the earth and in the sea, and all that is in them"* sing to the one seated on the throne and to the lamb (emphasis added)!

The lamb, of course, is Jesus, the priest and victim. The mixed metaphor becomes a theological reality! Three times in this chapter he is said to have been "slaughtered." That does not mean butchered or murdered. It is the word used in the Passover feast for the sacrifice of the Paschal lamb (Exodus 12:6). It also helps us to evoke the figure of the suffering servant in Isaiah 53 who was led like a lamb to the slaughter. Members of the Christian community were familiar with the designation of their savior as a lamb of sacrifice. John the Baptist had pointed him out: "He saw Jesus coming toward him and declared, 'Here is the Lamb of God who takes away the sin of the world!'" (John 1:29)

The scroll contains God's plan for history:

> With all wisdom and insight he has made known to us the mystery of his will, according to his good pleasure that he set forth in Christ, as a plan for the fullness of time, to gather up all things in him, things in heaven and things on earth. (Ephesians 1:9)

> ...the mystery that has been hidden throughout the ages and generations but has now been revealed to his saints. To them God chose to make known how great among the Gentiles are the riches of the glory of this mystery, which is Christ in you, the hope of glory. (Colossians 1:26)

> Without any doubt, the mystery of our religion is great:

> > He was revealed in flesh,
> >   vindicated in spirit,
> >   seen by angels,
> >   proclaimed among Gentiles,
> >   believed in throughout the world,
> >   taken up in glory. (1 Timothy 3:16)

> Long ago God spoke to our ancestors in many and various ways by the prophets, but in these last days he has spoken to us by a

Son, whom he appointed heir of all things, through whom he also created the world. He is the reflection of God's glory and the exact imprint of God's very being, and he sustains all things by his powerful word. When he had made purification for sins, he sat down at the right hand of the Majesty on high. (Hebrews 1:1–3)

And to give us a preview of coming attractions we can peek ahead to the author of Revelation's own vision of God's plan:

Then I saw heaven opened, and there was a white horse! Its rider is called Faithful and True, and in righteousness he judges and makes war. His eyes are like a flame of fire, and on his head are many diadems; and he has a name inscribed that no one knows but himself. He is clothed in a robe dipped in blood, and his name is called The Word of God. And the armies of heaven, wearing fine linen, white and pure, were following him on white horses. From his mouth comes a sharp sword with which to strike down the nations, and he will rule them with a rod of iron; he will tread the wine press of the fury of the wrath of God the Almighty. On his robe and on his thigh he has a name inscribed, "King of kings and Lord of lords." (Revelation 19:11–16)

REFLECTION

God's word, by whom all things were made, was Himself made flesh so that as perfect man He might save all and sum up all things in Himself. The Lord is the goal of human history, the focal point of the longings of history and of civilization, the center of the human race, the joy of every heart, and the answer to all its yearnings. He it is Whom the Father raised from the dead, lifted on high and stationed at His right hand, making Him judge of the living and the dead. Enlivened and united in His spirit, we journey toward the consummation of human history, one which fully accords with the counsel of God's love: "To reestablish all things in Christ, both those in the heavens and those on the earth" (Eph. 11:10). (*Gaudium et Spes*, 45)

CHAPTER SEVENTEEN

ACTS OF GOD? (6:1–8)

Then I saw the Lamb open one of the seven seals, and I heard one of the four living creatures call out, as with a voice of thunder, "Come!" I looked, and there was a white horse! Its rider had a bow; a crown was given to him, and he came out conquering and to conquer.

When he opened the second seal, I heard the second living creature call out, "Come!" And out came another horse, bright red; its rider was permitted to take peace from the earth, so that people would slaughter one another; and he was given a great sword.

When he opened the third seal, I heard the third living creature call out, "Come!" I looked, and there was a black horse! Its rider held a pair of scales in his hand, and I heard what seemed to be a voice in the midst of the four living creatures saying, "A quart of wheat for a day's pay, and three quarts of barley for a day's pay, but do not damage the olive oil and the wine!"

When he opened the fourth seal, I heard the voice of the fourth living creature call out, "Come!" I looked and there was a pale green horse! Its rider's name was Death, and Hades followed with him; they were given authority over a fourth of the earth, to kill with sword, famine, and pestilence, and by the wild animals of the earth. (6:1–9)

If you are the kind of person who rejoices at every tragedy that befalls guilty and innocent, every disaster that comes upon people indiscriminately, then this commentary is not for you. There are commentaries written by sensationalists who mistake the section of Revelation that begins now for a blueprint for the future. They take it as an exact description of the calamities that will befall us. According to them we now have an exact plan of the imminent unfolding of the details of history, as determined by God. It is nothing of the kind.

But to understand what it is, we have to ask what the author and his first hearers thought this litany of disasters was.

First of all, as people attentive to the Word of God, they knew that he consistently refused to reveal the future. They knew that he had forbidden them to seek out such information. "Do not turn to mediums or wizards; do not seek them out, to be defiled by them: I am the LORD your God" (Leviticus 19:31). "If any turn to mediums and wizards, prostituting themselves to them, I will set my face against them, and will cut them off from the people" (Leviticus 20:6). "A man or a woman who is a medium or a wizard shall be put to death; they shall be stoned to death, their blood is upon them" (Leviticus 20:27).

This prohibition against trying to find out what the future holds was taken so seriously that the heir of King Hezekiah, Manasseh, was considered the worst messiah the Jews ever had. Legend has it that he martyred the prophet Isaiah. Notice in the following passage that trying to find out about the future is so serious as to be condemned in the same breath as sacrificing his son to the pagan gods.

> Manasseh...did what was evil in the sight of the LORD, according to the abominable practices of the nations whom the LORD drove out before the people of Israel. For he rebuilt the high places that his father Hezekiah had pulled down, and erected altars to the Baals.... He built altars for all the host of heaven in the two courts of the house of the LORD. *He made his son pass through fire in the valley of the son of Hinnom, practiced soothsaying and augury and sorcery, and dealt with mediums and with wizards* [emphasis added]. He did much evil in the sight of the LORD, provoking him to anger. (2 Chronicles 33:1–6)

Jesus did not predict the future himself. But, like parents with their children, he threatened dire future consequences if they did not change their ways. He condemned in no uncertain terms those who claimed to be able to predict the future: "False messiahs and false prophets will appear and produce signs and omens, to lead astray, if possible, the elect" (Mark 13:22).

"But about that day or hour no one knows, neither the angels in heaven, nor the Son, but only the Father. Beware, keep alert; for you do not know when the time will come" (Mark 13:32). Isn't it amazing that the television evangelists of our time seem to have so much more information about the future than Jesus did?

Jesus told us what he thought of the people of his own time who were looking for reassurance about the future:

> This generation is an evil generation; it asks for a sign, but no sign will be given to it except the sign of Jonah. For just as Jonah became a sign to the people of Nineveh, so the Son of Man will be to this generation.... The people of Nineveh will rise up at the judgment with this generation and condemn it, because they repented at the proclamation of Jonah, and see, something greater than Jonah is here! (Luke 11:29–32)

Like all of the prophets before him, Jesus said that the best way to get ready for the future is not to know about it, but to convert and change your way of thinking and priorities.

But the scenario of the Book of Revelation is so detailed. Doesn't that indicate that the author had insider knowledge about the future? Not at all. He too, like all of the prophets before him, described the future in terms of the past. If they wanted to indicate how God would reward his people, they got their information from the "good old days." The future would be like Paradise, the Passover and the golden days of King David. And when they wanted information about how God would punish evildoers, they gathered their material from the "bad old days." The chaos that preceded creation, the plagues of the Exodus, the punishments that befell the unfaithful, the disasters that we call "acts of God" were all employed as stage props for an apocalyptic future.

The Books of Daniel, Ezekiel and Zechariah—prophets who were known for their prolific imaginations—provided the imagery and symbols that the author used.

To put it bluntly, this passage contains clues about the time in which it was written and very little, if any, history of the future. That is what the author intended, and that is why the first Christians understood him and his message.

There are two other points that need clarification:

1. The disasters are the work of God. All of the chaos bearing horses of this chapter, for instance, were sent by God. Nothing, but nothing, is out of his control, for he is the Pantocrator, the Omnipotent.

2. Hyperbole is rampant. As we just saw in 5:13: "Then I heard every creature in heaven and on earth and under the earth and in the sea, and all that is in them, singing, 'To the one seated on the throne and to the Lamb be blessing and honor and glory and might forever and ever!'"

If that were taken at face value, and the entire universe is doing what it is supposed to be doing—praising God—then there would be no reason for the writing of the Book of Revelation. If every creature praises God, there is nothing to be condemned and no punishment to be afraid of.

REFLECTION

John Henry Cardinal Newman wrote a challenging meditation on how God was active in his own life even when he was unaware of it:

> God has created me to do Him some definite service. He has committed some work to me that he has not committed to another. I have my mission—I may never know it in this life but I shall be told it in the next.... I am a link in a chain, a bond of connection between persons. He has not created me for naught. I shall do good, I shall do His work. I shall be an angel of peace, a preacher of truth in my own place, while not intending it, if I do but keep his commandments....

Therefore, I will trust Him. Whatever I am, I can never be thrown away. If I am in sickness, my sickness may serve Him. In perplexity, my perplexity may serve Him; if I am in sorrow, my sorrow may serve Him. He does nothing in vain.... He knows what he is about. He may take away my friends, he may throw me among strangers, he may make me feel desolate, make my spirits sink, hide my future from me—still He knows what He is about. (*Meditations and Devotions*, pp. 301–302)

CHAPTER EIGHTEEN

BITS AND PIECES

It is time to pause and examine some of the more esoteric passages or details that have been passed over in order to keep a perspective on the big picture.

"At once I was in the spirit" [or some translations: "in the Spirit"] (4:2).

Either the author is caught up in a deep mystical state or the Holy Spirit has taken hold of him and lifted him out of himself. This is a frequent prophetic experience. See Isaiah 6 where that prophet, too, is transported to a heavenly liturgy in a mystical state. In such a state the language and imagery are not of this world; hence, it is difficult for us who are of this world to comprehend easily and intelligibly.

In a sense he will be communicating with us in a different language and from a different point of reference than we are familiar with. To try to understand him only from our experience and not try to get into his shoes can only cause misunderstanding of what God is trying to tell us through him. For one thing, since he is in a prayerful state, he can only be understood by those who listen in a prayerful state, which is the purpose of this book.

"And out came another horse, bright red; its rider was permitted to take peace from the earth, so that people would slaughter one another; and he was given a great sword" (6:4).

Notice that the symbol of the four horsemen is borrowed from the prophet Zechariah. (Always check the footnotes and cross-references in your Bible, being mindful that the best commentary on the Bible is the Bible.)

The peace that is taken from the earth is removed not by some enemy, but by God who sent the red horse. This is another example of the Old Testament mentality that permeates the book. God is immediately responsible for everything that happens. This is obviously a primitive and simplistic point of view. It must be read with caution. To say that God allows some things to happen is not the same as taking the author's naïve point of view that God causes them to happen.

"A quart of wheat for a day's pay, and three quarts of barley for a day's pay, but do not damage the olive oil and the wine!" (6:5).

A famine is going on that will cause inflation and, as usual, will strike mostly at the working poor and the kind of food they consume. They will work all day just to fill their stomachs with barley, while the wheat, the wine and the oil will still be the prerogative of the privileged. Didn't someone say that the rich get richer and the poor get poorer?

"...every mountain and island was removed from its place" (6:14).

This is a bit more than rearranging the furniture in the parlor. It is the author's way of telling us that all the world's a stage and God is the director of this production.

"...and the stars of the sky fell to the earth as the fig tree drops its winter fruit" (6:23).

Just one star, even the smallest one, crashing into the earth would obliterate it completely. It would be total annihilation, which is certainly not going to happen since the whole object of the book is to get us ready for the Parousia. Where would Jesus come if the world is destroyed? But that's the problem of taking the author at face value, which he never intended.

The author is very fond of superlatives, including every creature of creation as glorifying God at one time and in another chapter being counted among his enemies:

> Look! He is coming with the clouds;
> *every* eye will see him,
> even those who pierced him;
> and on his account *all* the tribes of the earth
> will wail. (1:7) [emphasis added]

> Then I heard *every* creature in heaven and on earth and
> under the earth and in the sea, and *all* that is in them,
> singing,

"To the one seated on the throne and to the Lamb
be blessing and honor and glory and might
forever and ever!" (5:13) [emphasis added]

For you alone are holy.
All nations will come
and worship before you. (15:4) [emphasis added]

all the nations have drunk
of the wine of the wrath of her fornication. (18:3)
[emphasis added]

Then I saw an angel standing in the sun, and with a loud voice he
called to all the birds that fly in midheaven, "Come, gather for the
great supper of God, to eat the flesh of kings, the flesh of captains,
the flesh of the mighty, the flesh of horses and their riders—*flesh
of all, both free and slave, both small and great.* (19:17) [emphasis
added]

And is that no different from a person saying of a social event that "everyone was there" or tarring all the people of a nation with the same brush,
by declaring it an "evil empire"? If we stop and think we may find out that
some of the language of the Apocalypse is still our human way of getting
a point across.

REFLECTION

Those who are nervous or frightened by the work of serious
Biblical Scholarship betray their failure to grasp that marvelous
condescension of the Father who speaks in our ways. Many there
are and were who could not accept Jesus as coming from the
Father because he was too much like us. They predetermine how
God should manifest himself among us, and when that "image of
the Invisible God," does not fit their preconceived notions, they
turn from him. In like manner they would predetermine how
God may speak to us and look at the effort to determine the literary form and the intention of the author with suspicion. They

fail to realize that Biblical scholarship is not an attack on the truth, but a means to attain it. It does not obscure God's word but sheds light on it, for it respects it for what it is, the very word of God in words that are human. (from a homily of Humberto Cardinal Medeiros to a meeting of the Catholic Biblical Association)

CHAPTER NINETEEN

TURN THE OTHER CHEEK? (6:9–17)

When he opened the fifth seal, I saw under the altar the souls of those who had been slaughtered for the word of God and for the testimony they had given; they cried out with a loud voice, "Sovereign Lord, holy and true, how long will it be before you judge and avenge our blood on the inhabitants of the earth?" They were each given a white robe and told to rest a little longer, until the number would be complete both of their fellow ser-vantsand of their brothers and sisters, who were soon to be killed as they themselves had been killed.

When he opened the sixth seal, I looked, and there came a great earthquake; the sun became black as sackcloth, the full moon became like blood, and the stars of the sky fell to the earth as the fig tree drops its winter fruit when shaken by a gale. The sky vanished like a scroll rolling itself up, and every mountain and island was removed from its place. Then the kings of the earth and the magnates and the generals and the rich and the powerful, and everyone, slave and free, hid in the caves and among the rocks of the mountains, calling to the mountains and rocks, "Fall on us and hide us from the face of the one seated on the throne and from the wrath of the Lamb; for the great day of their wrath has come, and who is able to stand?"

The cry for vengeance, the counsel to rest until the number to be slaugh-tered would be complete (determined by God!), and the whole tone of the passage seem to reflect more the undeveloped morality that is associated with the Old Testament. There it is more readily understood, since they were more immature in their growth and development in morality. ("When Israel was a child, I loved him…" [Hosea 11:1].)

When such attitudes are found in the New Testament, however, they are a reflection of the identity crisis of the early Christian community. Very often when we think of the primitive church we only think of the community that Luke describes in the Acts of the Apostles:

> They devoted themselves to the apostles' teaching and fellowship, to the breaking of bread and the prayers. Awe came upon everyone, because many wonders and signs were being done by the apostles. All who believed were together and had all things in common; they would sell their possessions and goods and distribute the proceeds to all, as any had need. Day by day, as they spent much time together in the temple, they broke bread at home and ate their food with glad and generous hearts, praising God and having the goodwill of all the people. (Acts 2:42–47)

Luke's idealized portrait of what life was like in the early community is just that: idealized. The rest of the New Testament documents reflect the struggle of a community to find out what it meant to be a Christian. Jesus was a Jew and so were all of his followers. The only Bible they had was the Old Testament. Religious Jews were identified by how closely they adhered to it. And Matthew records Jesus as having said: "Do not think that I have come to abolish the law or the prophets; I have come not to abolish but to fulfill. For truly I tell you, until heaven and earth pass away, not one letter, not one stroke of a letter, will pass from the law until all is accomplished" (Matthew 5:17–18).

Eventually the community came to the realization that in his resurrection Jesus fulfilled and accomplished the plan of the Father. In him the new covenant or the New Testament had come. But the question of how much of the Old Testament was still valid and must be retained, and how much was superseded by the covenant in Jesus caused a great deal of tension.

The most obvious struggle was over the observance of the law. Paul was adamant that it had lost its binding force and he directly opposed Peter to his face in defense of our freedom from it. (See Paul's Letter to the Galatians, called the Magna Carta of Christianity.)

But that was only the most obvious struggle for Christian identity.

It was only by meditating on the Hebrew Scriptures that the community was able to discover the meaning of Jesus. All of his titles came from the Old Testament: Son of Man, Messiah, Redeemer, Shepherd, Paschal Lamb, Priest, Prophet. Once they had found them in the Old Testament, they had to ask whether Jesus had nuanced them or given them an entirely new connotation.

In this Book of Revelation we find an author who is still struggling to determine how Jesus had gone beyond the values, spirituality and morality of the Old Testament. He has not yet been able to emerge into the startling and challenging vision of Jesus that lays aside vindictiveness and vengeance.

Nor has he interiorized the values that we know from the Sermon on the Mount. That should not be surprising, since in many aspects we have not gotten much further than he did nineteen hundred years ago. Just read your daily papers!

REFLECTION

You have heard that it was said, "An eye for an eye and a tooth for a tooth." But I say to you, Do not resist an evildoer. But if anyone strikes you on the right cheek, turn the other also; and if anyone wants to sue you and take your coat, give your cloak as well; and if anyone forces you to go one mile, go also the second mile. Give to everyone who begs from you, and do not refuse anyone who wants to borrow from you.

You have heard that it was said, "You shall love your neighbor and hate your enemy." But I say to you, Love your enemies and pray for those who persecute you, so that you may be children of your Father in heaven; for he makes his sun rise on the evil and on the good, and sends rain on the righteous and on the unrighteous. For if you love those who love you, what reward do you have? Do not even the tax collectors do the same? And if you greet only your brothers and sisters, what more are you doing than others? Do not even the Gentiles do the same? Be perfect, therefore, as your heavenly Father is perfect. (Matthew 5:38–48) [Reflecting the struggle for Christian identity, Luke 6:36 uses "merciful" instead of "perfect"!]

CHAPTER TWENTY

ONLY 144,000? (7:1–17)

After this I saw four angels standing at the four corners of the earth, holding back the four winds of the earth so that no wind could blow on earth or sea or against any tree. I saw another angel ascending from the rising of the sun, having the seal of the living God, and he called with a loud voice to the four angels who had been given power to damage earth and sea, saying, "Do not damage the earth or the sea or the trees, until we have marked the servants of our God with a seal on their foreheads."

And I heard the number of those who were sealed, one hundred forty-four thousand, sealed out of every tribe of the people of Israel:

. . .

After this I looked, and there was a great multitude that no one could count, from every nation, from all tribes and peoples and languages, standing before the throne and before the Lamb, robed in white, with palm branches in their hands. They cried out in a loud voice, saying,

"Salvation belongs to our God who is seated on the throne, and to the Lamb!"

And all the angels stood around the throne and around the elders and the four living creatures, and they fell on their faces before the throne and worshiped God, singing,

Amen! Blessing and glory and wisdom
and thanksgiving and honor
and power and might
be to our God forever and ever! Amen.

Then one of the elders addressed me, saying, "Who are these, robed in white, and where have they come from?" I said to him,

"Sir, you are the one that knows." Then he said to me, "These are they who have come out of the great ordeal; they have washed their robes and made them white in the blood of the Lamb.

>For this reason they are before the throne of God,
>>and worship him day and night within his temple,
>>and the one who is seated on the throne will shelter them.
>
>They will hunger no more, and thirst no more;
>the sun will not strike them,
>nor any scorching heat;
>for the Lamb at the center of the throne will be their shepherd,
>and he will guide them to springs of the water of life,
>and God will wipe away every tear from their eyes."

When one is constantly using symbols to communicate truth, the message may get complicated and sometimes even amusing. For example, we are told that those in heaven will be exactly 144,000—no more, no less. However, a few lines later those in heaven are said to be a great multitude that no one could count. And it says they are going to stand before the Lamb. A spokesman for a sect that holds as a dogma that only 144,000 will be in heaven and insisted that it was literal and not a symbol, was asked if they would be in the presence of a little woolly lamb, as the text says. He insisted that the 144,000 in heaven must be calculated exactly and literally, but the lamb is a symbol! The sect wants it both ways. In reality, the truth behind the symbols is that Jesus desires all to be with him in heaven: "Now is the judgment of this world; now the ruler of this world will be driven out. And I, when I am lifted up from the earth, will draw all people to myself" (John 12:31–32). And in 5:13 the author himself insists that he heard not just 144,000, but "every creature in heaven and on earth and under the earth and in the sea, and all that is in them, singing, 'To the one seated on the throne and to the Lamb / be blessing and honor and glory and might / forever and ever!'"

Then the author mixes metaphors by having the saints make their robes white by washing them in blood! The imagery may be confused, but the message is clear: The washing is the cleansing of baptism made possible because Jesus offered his life (that is, his blood) in sacrifice. Paul's symbolism of death and resurrection expresses the same truth a little more clearly:

> Do you not know that all of us who have been baptized into Christ Jesus were baptized into his death? Therefore we have been buried with him by baptism into death, so that, just as Christ was raised from the dead by the glory of the Father, so we too might walk in newness of life.
>
> For if we have been united with him in a death like his, we will certainly be united with him in a resurrection like his. We know that our old self was crucified with him so that the body of sin might be destroyed, and we might no longer be enslaved to sin. For whoever has died is freed from sin. But if we have died with Christ, we believe that we will also live with him. We know that Christ, being raised from the dead, will never die again; death no longer has dominion over him. The death he died, he died to sin, once for all; but the life he lives, he lives to God. So you also must consider yourselves dead to sin and alive to God in Christ Jesus. (Romans 6:3–11)

And then the author really mixes his metaphors. He makes the lamb into a shepherd! The author is sure that we will get the point. The Lord Jesus Christ is priest and victim. He is both the gift sacrificed and the one who offers it on behalf of the flock. He is both Sheep and Shepherd. The third preface of Easter goes a step further and also makes him the altar: "As he offered his body on the cross, his perfect sacrifice fulfilled all others. As he gave himself into your hands for our salvation, he showed himself to be the priest, the altar and the lamb of sacrifice."

REFLECTION

Go therefore and make disciples of all nations, baptizing them in the name of the Father and of the Son and of the Holy Spirit.... (Matthew 28:19)

In him all the fullness of God was pleased to dwell, and through him God was pleased to reconcile to himself all things, whether on earth or in heaven, by making peace through the blood of his cross. (Colossians 1:19–20)

This is right and is acceptable in the sight of God our Savior, who desires everyone to be saved and to come to the knowledge of the truth. For there is one God; there is also one mediator between God and humankind, Christ Jesus, himself human, who gave himself a ransom for all. (1 Timothy 2:3–6)

For the grace of God has appeared, bringing salvation to all, training us to renounce impiety and worldly passions, and in the present age to live lives that are self-controlled, upright, and godly, while we wait for the blessed hope and the manifestation of the glory of our great God and Savior, Jesus Christ. (Titus 2:11–13)

CHAPTER TWENTY-ONE

DIVINE MERCY (8:1–13)

When the Lamb opened the seventh seal, there was silence in heaven for about half an hour. And I saw the seven angels who stand before God, and seven trumpets were given to them.

Another angel with a golden censer came and stood at the altar; he was given a great quantity of incense to offer with the prayers of all the saints on the golden altar that is before the throne. And the smoke of the incense, with the prayers of the saints, rose before God from the hand of the angel. Then the angel took the censer and filled it with fire from the altar and threw it on the earth; and there were peals of thunder, rumblings, flashes of lightning, and an earthquake.

Now the seven angels who had the seven trumpets made ready to blow them.

The first angel blew his trumpet, and there came hail and fire, mixed with blood, and they were hurled to the earth; and *a third* of the earth was burned up, and *a third* of the trees were burned up, and all green grass was burned up.

The second angel blew his trumpet, and something like a great mountain, burning with fire, was thrown into the sea. *A third* of the sea became blood, *a third* of the living creatures in the sea died, and *a third* of the ships were destroyed.

The third angel blew his trumpet, and a great star fell from heaven, blazing like a torch, and it fell on *a third* of the rivers and on the springs of water. The name of the star is Wormwood. *A third* of the waters became wormwood, and many died from the water, because it was made bitter.

The fourth angel blew his trumpet, and *a third* of the sun was struck, and *a third* of the moon, and *a third* of the stars, so that *a third* of their light was darkened; a third of the day was kept from shining, and likewise the night.

> Then I looked, and I heard an eagle crying with a loud voice
> as it flew in midheaven, "Woe, woe, woe to the inhabitants of the
> earth, at the blasts of the other trumpets that the three angels are
> about to blow!" [emphasis added]

Two things must be kept in mind if we are to make sense of this chapter. First we must remember that the Bible is filled with anthropomorphisms, which are nothing less than making God in our own image and likeness. We act and speak as if God acts and speaks just we do. He does not (even to call God *he* is an anthropomorphism). God is holy, and holy means totally different, completely other.

There is no doubt that there are plenty of texts in the Old Testament to support those who conclude that it manifests a God of anger, violence and bloodshed. But those are the texts in which an angry, desperate and persecuted people attribute to God their own feelings and reactions. While we have only human language in which to speak to and refer to God, we must step back and realize that God is not like us; he doesn't react the way we would. Isaiah had to remind his people of the difference between creator and creature:

> Seek the LORD while he may be found,
>> call upon him while he is near;
> let the wicked forsake their way,
>> and the unrighteous their thoughts;
> let them return to the LORD, that he may have mercy on them,
>> and to our God, for he will abundantly pardon.
> For my thoughts are not your thoughts,
>> nor are your ways my ways, says the LORD.
> For as the heavens are higher than the earth,
>> so are my ways higher than your ways
>> and my thoughts than your thoughts. (Isaiah 55:6–9)

Secondly, we can only appreciate Hebrew thought when we realize that the Semitic peoples often aren't comfortable with speculation and abstraction. They tend to prefer stories to definitions, and examples to abstruse discourse. It is for this reason that Jesus does not define love, but tells the shocking story of the Good Samaritan. If you don't know what love is after hearing that parable, no explanation is possible.

With these two principles in mind we can begin to comprehend the real truth of chapter eight. It is about divine mercy! God "will not execute his fierce anger." He is a God of mercy and compassion, not of vindictiveness and revenge. He is not like us. And the best way for the author to get his point across concretely is to affirm that God will not obliterate everything and everyone. He won't even annihilate one half. The one-third that is destroyed is meant to highlight the two-thirds that survive, thanks to God's divine mercy. Contrary to all appearances, it is a message of hope.

REFLECTION
Those who can find in the Hebrew Scriptures only a God of unremitting anger and vengeance have indeed perused it selectively as the following from Isaiah 54:5–7 clearly shows.

> For your Maker is your husband,
> the LORD of hosts is his name;
> the Holy One of Israel is your Redeemer,
> the God of the whole earth he is called.
> For the LORD has called you
> like a wife forsaken and grieved in spirit,
> like the wife of a man's youth when she is cast off,
> says your God.
> For a brief moment I abandoned you,
> but with great compassion I will gather you.

CHAPTER TWENTY-TWO

HITTING BOTTOM (9:1–21)

And the fifth angel blew his trumpet, and I saw a star that had fallen from heaven to earth, and he was given the key to the shaft of the bottomless pit; he opened the shaft of the bottomless pit, and from the shaft rose smoke like the smoke of a great furnace, and the sun and the air were darkened with the smoke from the shaft. Then from the smoke came locusts on the earth, and they were given authority like the authority of scorpions of the earth. They were told not to damage the grass of the earth or any green growth or any tree, but only those people who do not have the seal of God on their foreheads. They were allowed to torture them for five months, but not to kill them, and their torture was like the torture of a scorpion when it stings someone. And in those days people will seek death but will not find it; they will long to die, but death will flee from them.

In appearance the locusts were like horses equipped for battle. On their heads were what looked like crowns of gold; their faces were like human faces, their hair like women's hair, and their teeth like lions' teeth; they had scales like iron breastplates, and the noise of their wings was like the noise of many chariots with horses rushing into battle. They have tails like scorpions, with stingers, and in their tails is their power to harm people for five months. They have as king over them the angel of the bottomless pit; his name in Hebrew is *Abaddon*, and in Greek he is called *Apollyon*.

The first woe has passed. There are still two woes to come.

Then the sixth angel blew his trumpet, and I heard a voice from the fourhorns of the golden altar before God, saying to the sixth angel who had the trumpet, "Release the four angels who are bound at the great river Euphrates." So the four angels were released, who had been held ready for the hour, the day, the month, and the year, to kill a third of humankind. The number of the troops of cavalry was two hundred million; I heard their number. And this was how I saw the horses in my vision: the riders wore breastplates the color of fire and of sapphire and of sulfur; the heads of the horses were like lions' heads, and fire and smoke and sulfur came out of their mouths. By these three plagues a third of humankind was killed, by the fire and smoke and sulfur coming out of their mouths. For the power of the horses is in their mouths and in their tails; their tails are like serpents, having heads; and with them they inflict harm.

The rest of humankind, who were not killed by these plagues, did not repent of the works of their hands or give up worshiping demons and idols of gold and silver and bronze and stone and wood, which cannot see or hear or walk. And they did not repent of their murders or their sorceries or their fornication or their thefts.

When the prophets wanted to comfort the afflicted by expressing what the future would be like, they mined the Scriptures for examples from the good old days. Thus, Isaiah has in mind the tranquility of Paradise as he speaks of the lion who will lie down with the lamb. It is not to be taken too literally. As someone suggested, the lamb should pray that the lion is a vegetarian!

When the prophets who specialized in apocalyptic writings wanted to "afflict the comfortable," they looked in the Scriptures for curses, disasters, plagues and every tragedy that would shock and wake up their people. In this chapter there is a litany of disasters so horrific that we must admire the imagination of the author. He assembles a horror show that would do any Hollywood producer proud. If you were a person who was living a self-centered life apart from God, literally a self-made person, you would probably hear of these tragedies and say, "I'll be good!"

It is all the more amazing then that the author proclaims twice, "They did not repent. They did not repent." Their stubbornness and hardness of heart seem almost beyond belief. The evil is not so much in the cosmic tragedies as in the hearts of the people. As a partial explanation, he invokes the malevolent presence of Abbadon, the closest the Bible comes to speaking of what we would call the power of hell. But he goes out of his way to give its Greek translation: *Apollyon*. It sounds decidedly like *Apollo*, the pagan god with which the evil Roman Emperor Domitian, who persecuted Christians, identified.

His readers would not miss the allusion. Domitian was malevolent enough, but beyond the Euphrates lay the bloodthirsty Parthian hordes, always with their armies like a plague of locusts. So the author marshals biblical disaster and adds impending military destruction by the barbarians to describe what is the opposite of the kingdom of God. Which is worse? The devil you know or the devil you don't know? The scenario doesn't answer the question, but invokes both of them, and in incredulity and total exasperation, the author laments, "they did not repent...they did not repent."

REFLECTION

Alcoholics refer to "hitting bottom," the devastating awareness that their life is hell and they have lost all control; that they are so far down that there is no place to fall but on their knees and there is nowhere to look but up. Sometimes others may be instrumental in bringing them or us to that awareness. There is no recovery without hitting bottom, as painful as that may be. Our author is trying to facilitate hitting bottom for his readers that they might repent, realize how helpless they are, and turn to the Lord.

CHAPTER TWENTY-THREE

THE PAUSE THAT REFRESHES (10:1–4)

And I saw another mighty angel coming down from heaven, wrapped in a cloud, with a rainbow over his head; his face was like the sun, and his legs like pillars of fire. He held a little scroll open in his hand. Setting his right foot on the sea and his left foot on the land, he gave a great shout, like a lion roaring. And when he shouted, the seven thunders sounded. And when the seven thunders had sounded, I was about to write, but I heard a voice from heaven saying, "Seal up what the seven thunders have said, and do not write it down."

In the early church the followers of Marcion were so turned off by the violence, vengeance and chaos that seem to mark the history of Israel, that they came to the conclusion that the love and mercy so prevalent in the New Testament meant that there were two separate Gods. They could not imagine how the Father of Jesus could in any way be identified with what they perceived as the angry, arbitrary, unloving and unmerciful God that seemed to them to inhabit the Old Testament. The theory of the Marcionites is not just a historical curiosity. Those who read the Old Testament uncritically and superficially today are kindred spirits.

Marcion and company missed the underlying themes of the Old Testament: Yahweh's love and mercy. When Yahweh appeared to Moses at the time of the giving of the Decalogue, he implies that the meaning of his very name is synonymous with love and mercy.

The LORD descended in the cloud and stood with him there, and proclaimed the name, "The LORD" [Yahweh]. The LORD [Yahweh] passed before him, and proclaimed,
"The LORD, the LORD, [Yahweh, Yahweh]
a God merciful and gracious,
slow to anger,

> and abounding in steadfast love and faithfulness,
>
>   keeping steadfast love for the thousandth generation,
>
>   forgiving iniquity and transgression and sin....
>
> (Exodus 34:5–7)

And when Jesus was asked which was the greatest commandment of the law, he did not give a new one. He quoted Deuteronomy. This is the Shamah, or creed of Israel, which was in the phylacteries on their arms and the mezuzahs on their doorposts.

> "Hear, O Israel: The LORD is our God, the LORD alone. You shall love the LORD your God with all your heart, and with all your soul, and with all your might. Keep these words that I am commanding you today in your heart. (Deuteronomy 6:4)

The Psalms are a compendium of the spirituality of the Old Testament. In them Yahweh's vengeance is mentioned four times but his love, over one hundred and fifty times!

> Be mindful of your mercy, O LORD, and of your steadfast love,
>
>   for they have been from of old.
>
> Do not remember the sins of my youth or my transgressions;
>
>   according to your steadfast love remember me,
>
> for your goodness' sake, O LORD! (Psalm 25:6, 7)

> All the paths of the LORD are steadfast love and faithfulness,
>
>   for those who keep his covenant and his decrees. (Psalm 25:10)

Even in the tragic and devastating Babylonian exile, at a time when they often felt abandoned by God, his people did not despair: "The steadfast love of the LORD never ceases, his mercies never come to an end.... Although he causes grief, he will have compassion according to the abundance of his steadfast love; for he does not willingly afflict or grieve anyone" (Lamentations 3:22, 32–33).

Perhaps the most touching example of Yahweh's love and forgiveness is that of the tragic love of the prophet Hosea for his unfaithful wife. He will recapture "the love you had at first" (cf., for a comparison the letter to Ephesus in Revelation). Both Hosea and Yahweh will do this by taking their spouses on a second honeymoon.

All of this is to put us in a frame of mind for understanding chapter ten. In the midst of all the chaos, God sends a special angel with a message of love and mercy. It straddles earth, sea and sky. It is signified by the cloud, the sign of his protective glory, by the rainbow, the sign of his faithful and everlasting covenant; by the sun, which also radiated from the face of the risen one who lives forever and ever (1:16); and by the pillars of the cloud that guided God's people from slavery to freedom. Impeccable credentials!

And while he bears a revelation from God the seer is told not to make it known. It can only be because the author perceives God as having second thoughts. Saint Mark (13:20–27) in his own "little apocalypse" has Jesus talking about a similar respite: "And if the Lord had not cut short those days, no one would be saved; but for the sake of the elect, whom he chose, he has cut short those days."

This concept of the omnipotent, unchanging God, sometimes changing his mind is found throughout the Old Testament. In Exodus 32 God loses his patience with the Israelites who set up the golden calf. He decides to wipe them out and start all over. In a marvelous (and humorous) example of biblical prayer, Moses asks God if he has considered how foolish he will look in the eyes of the Egyptians. He led the Israelites out of Egypt and then appeared to have lost his steam when they disappeared in the desert. Yahweh admits that he hadn't seen that aspect from Moses' point of view and grants a respite to his people. Prayer works!

In one of the loveliest passages of the Old Testament, Yahweh changes his mind about abandoning his recalcitrant people. It is not in him to do so, because of his compassion. A mere human being might give up, but not God!

> How can I give you up, Ephraim?
> How can I hand you over, O Israel?
> ...

My heart recoils within me;
>   my compassion grows warm and tender.
I will not execute my fierce anger;
>   I will not again destroy Ephraim;
for I am God and no mortal,
>   the Holy One in your midst,
>   and I will not come in wrath. (Hosea 11:8–9)

REFLECTION

It is this long-suffering Father that Jesus reveals to us in this parable.

Then Jesus said, "There was a man who had two sons. The younger of them said to his father, 'Father, give me the share of the property that will belong to me.' So he divided his property between them. A few days later the younger son gathered all he had and traveled to a distant country, and there he squandered his property in dissolute living. When he had spent everything, a severe famine took place throughout that country, and he began to be in need. So he went and hired himself out to one of the citizens of that country, who sent him to his fields to feed the pigs. He would gladly have filled himself with the pods that the pigs were eating; and no one gave him anything. But when he came to himself he said, 'How many of my father's hired hands have bread enough and to spare, but here I am dying of hunger! I will get up and go to my father, and I will say to him, "Father, I have sinned against heaven and before you; I am no longer worthy to be called your son; treat me like one of your hired hands."' So he set off and went to his father. But while he was still far off, his father saw him and was filled with compassion; he ran and put his arms around him and kissed him. Then the son said to him, 'Father, I have sinned against heaven and before you; I am no longer worthy to be called your son.' But the father said to his slaves, 'Quickly, bring out a robe—the best one—and put it on him; put a ring on his finger and sandals on his feet. And get the fatted calf and kill it, and let us eat and celebrate; for this son of mine was dead and is alive again; he was lost and is found!' And they began to celebrate.

Now his elder son was in the field; and when he came and approached the house, he heard music and dancing. He called one of the slaves and asked what was going on. He replied, 'Your brother has come, and your father has killed the fatted calf, because he has got him back safe and sound.' Then he became angry and refused to go in. His father came out and began to plead with him. But he answered his father, 'Listen! For all these years I have been working like a slave for you, and I have never disobeyed your command; yet you have never given me even a young goat so that I might celebrate with my friends. But when this son of yours came back, who has devoured your property with prostitutes, you killed the fatted calf for him!' Then the father said to him, 'Son, you are always with me, and all that is mine is yours. But we had to celebrate and rejoice, because this brother of yours was dead and has come to life; he was lost and has been found.'" (Luke 15:11–32)

CHAPTER TWENTY-FOUR

GOD'S WORD AND INDIGESTION (10:5–11)

Then the angel whom I saw standing on the sea and the land
    raised his right hand to heaven
    and swore by him who lives forever and ever,
who created heaven and what is in it, the earth and what is in it,
and the sea and what is in it: "There will be no more delay, but in
the days when the seventh angel is to blow his trumpet, the mystery of God will be fulfilled, as he announced to his servants the
prophets."

Then the voice that I had heard from heaven spoke to me
again, saying, "Go, take the scroll that is open in the hand of the
angel who is standing on the sea and on the land." So I went to
the angel and told him to give me the little scroll; and he said to
me, "Take it, and eat; it will be bitter to your stomach, but sweet
as honey in your mouth." So I took the little scroll from the hand
of the angel and ate it; it was sweet as honey in my mouth, but
when I had eaten it, my stomach was made bitter.

Then they said to me, "You must prophesy again about many
peoples and nations and languages and kings."

Chronology takes on a new dimension as the power of God continues to
be manifested in a universe that he made and called "good." Dozing in the
back seat of a car, little children may ask, "Are we there yet?" They quickly
wake up when the voice from the front seat says: "We're there; we have
arrived." In saying that "there will be no more delay" the angel is really
talking about history that's in progress. We have arrived!

The author is in the great tradition of the prophets who have gone
before him and, like a new Jeremiah, his judgment is upon "many peoples
and nations and languages and kings." "Before I formed you in the womb
I knew you, / and before you were born I consecrated you; / I appointed
you a prophet to the nations"(Jeremiah 1:5).

But anyone who accepts the role of a prophet knows that proclaiming "the mystery of God" is bittersweet. Again, Jeremiah is the role model:

> [You Yahweh,] know that on your account I suffer insult.
> Your words were found, and I ate them,
>> and your words became to me a joy
>> and the delight of my heart;
> for I am called by your name,
>> O LORD, God of hosts. (Jeremiah 15:15–16)

But that euphoria does not last long. Jeremiah soon finds out that Yahweh never promised him a rose garden.

> O LORD, you have enticed me,
>> and I was enticed;
> you have overpowered me,
>> and you have prevailed.
> I have become a laughingstock all day long;
>> everyone mocks me.
> For whenever I speak, I must cry out,
>> I must shout, "Violence and destruction!"
> For the word of the LORD has become for me
>> a reproach and derision all day long.
> If I say, "I will not mention him,
>> or speak any more in his name,"
> then within me there is something like a burning fire
>> shut up in my bones;
> I am weary with holding it in,
>> and I cannot. (Jeremiah 20:7–9)

The translator very delicately translates the Hebrew word for *seduce*, as *entice*. The image of how Jeremiah feels about being a prophet is that of a virgin seduced by a man with the promise of marriage, only to be dropped when he gets her pregnant.

And Jesus, although he much preferred the title *Prophet* to *Messiah*, had no delusions about what the job description involved. "He said to them, 'Doubtless you will quote to me this proverb, "Doctor, cure yourself." And you will say, "Do here also in your hometown the things that we have heard you did at Capernaum."' And he said, 'Truly I tell you, no prophet is accepted in the prophet's hometown'" (Luke 4:23).

The bitterness that comes from being a prophet is that one suffers rejection at the hands of those one loves the most. Prophets only criticize so much because they love so much. They see promise unfulfilled, potential not lived up to, in those whom they love and are disturbed enough to name the problem, to unmask the idol. And that can bring a violent reaction from those criticized.

Jesus knew that better than any prophet before or since. And he warned his disciples that they were not greater than the master. His fate would be theirs because it went with the territory. "Blessed are you when people revile you and persecute you and utter all kinds of evil against you falsely on my account. Rejoice and be glad, for your reward is great in heaven, for in the same way they persecuted the prophets who were before you" (Matthew 5:11–12).

REFLECTION

John Gardner, the founder of Common Cause, once depicted himself as an archaeologist of the twenty-fifth century casting his eyes over the ruins of our own twenty-first century civilization. Inquiring what happened to it, he answers his own question. "At the beginning of the twenty-first century there emerged two kinds of people: uncritical lovers and unloving critics. The first were blind to the malignancies in our culture which they smothered in an embrace of blind love. The second group were those who had no love and could only criticize, cynically and negatively. Between the two groups our civilization and all of its institutions perished."

But Gardner failed to mention a third group: those who could save even a dying civilization. They are the loving critics and critical lovers, also known as prophets. In the midst of smugness and self-satisfaction, they recognize promise unfulfilled and potential unrealized. And they criticize unmercifully. And that is only because they love so much.

CHAPTER TWENTY-FIVE

THE TWO WITNESSES (11:1–14)

Then I was given a measuring rod like a staff, and I was told, "Come and measure the temple of God and the altar and those who worship there, but do not measure the court outside the temple; leave that out, for it is given over to the nations, and they will trample over the holy city for forty-two months. And I will grant my two witnesses authority to prophesy for one thousand two hundred sixty days, wearing sackcloth."

These are the two olive trees and the two lampstands that stand before the Lord of the earth. And if anyone wants to harm them, fire pours from their mouth and consumes their foes; anyone who wants to harm them must be killed in this manner. They have authority to shut the sky, so that no rain may fall during the days of their prophesying, and they have authority over the waters to turn them into blood, and to strike the earth with every kind of plague, as often as they desire.

When they have finished their testimony, the beast that comes up from the bottomless pit will make war on them and conquer them and kill them, and their dead bodies will lie in the street of the great city that is prophetically called Sodom and Egypt, where also their Lord was crucified. For three and a half days members of the peoples and tribes and languages and nations will gaze at their dead bodies and refuse to let them be placed in a tomb; and the inhabitants of the earth will gloat over them and celebrate and exchange presents, because these two prophets had been a torment to the inhabitants of the earth.

But after the three and a half days, the breath of life from God entered them, and they stood on their feet, and those who saw them were terrified. Then they heard a loud voice from heaven saying to them, "Come up here!" And they went up to heaven in a cloud while their enemies watched them. At that moment there was a great earthquake, and a tenth of the city fell; seven thousand people were killed in the earthquake, and the rest were terrified and gave glory to the God of heaven.

The second woe has passed. The third woe is coming very soon.

This chapter is one of the most deeply symbolic and esoteric thus far. As in the rest of the book, none of the symbols are to be taken literally or at face value. And so:

- Rome is not (just) Rome but every city of the Roman Empire.
- Jerusalem (already destroyed at the time of writing) is not just the historical city but every city where the Lord is crucified in his Body, the church.
- The two witnesses are not (just) Moses and Elijah but every faithful Christian.
- 1,260 days or three and a half (days or years) or forty-two months are not to be calculated by the calendar. They are the period of chaos when Antiochus Epiphanes set up the Abomination of the Desolation in the Holy of Holies in the temple (167–164 B.C.). At the end of that time God triumphed through the hands of the Maccabees who re-consecrated the temple and established the feast of lights (Hanukkah).

Without going into every detail of every symbol, we may summarize and paraphrase the message of these chapters thus:

I was mandated to mark and consecrate as God's own, the church, God's people, who are set apart as cooperators in his plan. In all of the Roman Empire, a period of persecution is raging. During it the faithful will bear prophetic witness. They are in the tradition of the priest and prophet of old shining in the presence of the Lord. For the moment no one can touch them. To them has been given the power to work the great signs in the pattern of Moses and Elijah. But when they have completed their role of witnessing, the power of the Roman Empire will seem to prevail and they will have neither a decent death nor burial (like their Lord) whether in Sodom, Egypt, Jerusalem, Rome or any city where the faithful may be found in the Empire. The disciples are not greater than the Master and they will suffer the same fate as Jesus. They will be despised by the rest of the inhabitants of the earth who violently resented and took umbrage at their prophetic witness. But God will not be mocked, for he will do for the church what he did for his Son. And when he brings her to himself, her persecutors will stand looking up with their mouths open. This cosmic event is (was? will be?) witnessed by the groaning of creation, with a large number perishing in the cataclysm. Those left behind begin to think twice about their priorities and start to sing a different tune. Praise God!

REFLECTION

I consider that the sufferings of this present time are not worth comparing with the glory about to be revealed to us. For the creation waits with eager longing for the revealing of the children of God; for the creation was subjected to futility, not of its own will but by the will of the one who subjected it, in hope that the creation itself will be set free from its bondage to decay and will obtain the freedom of the glory of the children of God. We know that the whole creation has been groaning in labor pains until now; and not only the creation, but we ourselves, who have the first fruits of the Spirit, groan inwardly while we wait for adoption, the redemption of our bodies. For in hope we were saved. Now hope that is seen is not hope. For who hopes for what is seen But if we hope for what we do not see, we wait for it with patience. (Romans 8:18–25)

CHAPTER TWENTY-SIX

GOD'S POINT OF VIEW (11:15–19)

Then the seventh angel blew his trumpet, and there were loud voices in heaven, saying,

> "The kingdom of the world has become the kingdom of our
>   Lord
>   and of his Messiah
>   and he will reign forever and ever."

Then the twenty-four elders who sit on their thrones before God fell on their faces and worshiped God, singing,

> "We give you thanks, Lord God Almighty,
>   who are and who were,
>   for you have taken your great power
>   and begun to reign.
> The nations raged,
>   but your wrath has come,
>   and the time for judging the dead,
>   for rewarding your servants the prophets
>   and saints and all who fear your name,
>   both small and great,
>   and for destroying those who destroy the earth."

Then God's temple in heaven was opened, and the ark of his covenant was seen within his temple; and there were flashes of lightning, rumblings, peals of thunder, an earthquake, and heavy hail.

Perhaps the most appropriate setting for appreciating this passage is its place in the *Messiah*. Along with verses 19:6, 16 (King James version) Handel incorporated the passage into the immortal "Alleluia Chorus":

> Hallelujah! for the Lord God Omnipotent reigneth!
> The kingdom of this world is become the kingdom of our

Lord, and of His Christ; and he shall reign forever and ever.
King of Kings, and Lord of Lords.
Hallelujah!

Once again, time is telescoped. Past, present and future are indistinguishable because we are to see things from God's perspective in eternity where there are no clocks or calendars. With chaos raging around him, and the worst yet to come, the author helps us to catch our breath by drawing us into the heavenly liturgy where our twenty-four stand-ins or understudies in the divine drama glorify God who has triumphed (even though there are a few chapters yet to go!).

From his perspective the separation of church and state has no meaning. It is either Christ or Caesar: "No one can serve two masters." When Jesus is all in all, and the church's plea "thy kingdom come, thy will be done, on earth as it is in heaven" is answered, then all will be the "kingdom of our Lord and of his Christ."

But before that can be celebrated, justice and peace must prevail. That can only happen if there is, as in all liturgies, a rite of reconciliation. For the cosmic liturgy, that will be a final cosmic judgment. Those for whom there has been no justice must be vindicated, and those who thought of themselves as the movers and shakers will be seen for what they really were: "destroyers of the earth."

Barbara Tuchman, in her book *The Proud Tower: A Portrait of the World Before the War, 1890–1914,* paints a vivid picture of the need for such a judgment in an unjust world: "Most of those from whom anarchists of the deed were made were voiceless or could speak their protest only in the wail of a dispossessed Irish peasant spading his field for the last time, who was asked by a visitor what he wanted. 'What is it I am wantin'?' cried the old man, shaking his fist at the sky. 'I want the Day [of] Judgment!'

The indication that we are in a whole new framework and operation is the opening of the heavenly temple and the public manifestation of the Ark of the Covenant. Before it was destroyed or lost at the first destruction of Jerusalem by the Babylonians in 587 B.C., the ark was seen only by the high priest on one day of the year—Yom Kippur, the day of Atonement.

It was the sign of God's presence among his people and his reconciling them to himself (*at-one-ment*). Now, since the great High Priest has assimilated them into his own priesthood, (1:6, 5:10, 20:6) they can look up and see the ark, confirming that they are not alone.

> But when Christ came as a high priest of the good things that have come, then through the greater and more perfect tent [tabernacle] (not made with hands, that is, not of this creation), he entered once for all into the Holy Place, not with the blood of goats and calves, but with his own blood, thus obtaining eternal redemption (Hebrews 9:11–12).

> Therefore, my friends, since we have confidence to enter the sanctuary by the blood of Jesus, by the new and living way that he opened for us through the curtain (that is, through his flesh), and since we have a great priest over the house of God, let us approach with a true heart in full assurance of faith, with our hearts sprinkled clean from an evil conscience and our bodies washed with pure water. Let us hold fast to the confession of our hope without wavering, for he who has promised is faithful. (Hebrews 10:19)

REFLECTION

Father, all powerful and ever-living God,
We do well always and everywhere to give you thanks.
You anointed Jesus Christ, your only son, with the oil of gladness,
as the eternal priest and king.
As priest he offered his life on the altar of the cross and redeemed
the human race by this one perfect sacrifice of peace.
As King he claims dominion over all creation,
that he may present to you, his almighty Father
An eternal and universal kingdom:
A kingdom of truth and life,
A kingdom of holiness and grace,
A kingdom of justice, love and peace.
(preface of Christ the King)

CHAPTER TWENTY-SEVEN

THE WOMAN CLOTHED WITH THE SUN
(12:1–6, 13–17)

A great portent appeared in heaven: a woman clothed with the sun, with the moon under her feet, and on her head a crown of twelve stars. She was pregnant and was crying out in birth pangs, in the agony of giving birth. Then another portent appeared in heaven: a great red dragon, with seven heads and ten horns, and seven diadems on his heads. His tail swept down a third of the stars of heaven and threw them to the earth. Then the dragon stood before the woman who was about to bear a child, so that he might devour her child as soon as it was born. And she gave birth to a son, a male child, who is to rule all the nations with a rod of iron. But her child was snatched away and taken to God and to his throne; and the woman fled into the wilderness, where she has a place prepared by God, so that there she can be nourished for one thousand two hundred sixty days.

. . .

So when the dragon saw that he had been thrown down to the earth, he pursued the woman who had given birth to the male child. But the woman was given the two wings of the great eagle, so that she could fly from the serpent into the wilderness, to her place where she is nourished for a time, and times, and half a time. Then from his mouth the serpent poured water like a river after the woman, to sweep her away with the flood. But the earth came to the help of the woman; it opened its mouth and swallowed the river that the dragon had poured from his mouth. Then the dragon was angry with the woman, and went off to make war on the rest of her children, those who keep the commandments of God and hold the testimony of Jesus.

(The Book of Revelation was written over a period of thirty years at least. During that time many additions, insertions, elaborations and explanations became part of the inspired text. The heavenly war is one such interpolation and will be dealt with in the next chapter.)

Of all the rich symbols in the Apocalypse, this sign or portent is the richest and most multifaceted. Catholics have perhaps been programmed by the liturgies for the feasts of the Immaculate Conception and the Assumption to identify the woman immediately as Mary. Although this passage offers no proof for Marian dogmas, it certainly does refer to Mary, the Mother of Christ (the Messiah). To appreciate the richness of the symbolism, it is necessary to keep in mind that the author sees her in the light of *the woman* of Genesis 3:14–16:

> "The LORD God said to the serpent,
>
> ...
>
>> I will put enmity between you and the woman,
>>> and between your offspring and hers;
>> he will strike your head,
>>> and you will strike his heel."
>> To the woman he said,
>> "I will greatly increase your pangs in childbearing;
>>> in pain you shall bring forth children...."

Nor should one forget her cosmic dimension, which is already implied in the predestination of her Son. "Blessed be the God and Father of our Lord Jesus Christ, who has blessed us in Christ with every spiritual blessing in the heavenly places, just as he chose us in Christ before the foundation of the world to be holy and blameless before him in love" (Ephesians 1:3–4).

We do not often think of Mary suffering the pains of labor, but every woman does. It is part of the natural process. We do give her the title of Mother of Sorrows, recognizing that she was no stranger to the suffering that is a part of life. She was not exempt from any aspect of the fullness of humanity that her Son embraced.

Therefore, he had to become like his brothers and sisters in every respect, so that he might be a merciful and faithful high priest in the service of God, to make a sacrifice of atonement for the sins of the people. Because he himself was tested by what he suffered, he is able to help those who are being tested. (Hebrews 2:17–18)

LIKE SON, LIKE MOTHER!

If it seems odd that her child is glorified in heaven immediately after his birth, this is just the author's way of proclaiming that he is the Messiah. Among God's people the Messiah's birthday was not the actual date of birth. It was the day of his enthronement as Messiah, as Psalm 2, sung at his coronation makes abundantly clear: "I have set my king on Zion, my holy hill." / I will tell of the decree of the LORD: / He said to me, "You are my son; / today I have begotten you." It is this custom that allows us to make sense of Paul's greeting to the Romans: "Paul, a servant of Jesus Christ, called to be an apostle, set apart for the gospel of God, which he promised beforehand through his prophets in the holy scriptures, the gospel concerning his Son, who was descended from David according to the flesh and was declared to be Son of God with power according to the spirit of holiness by resurrection from the dead, Jesus Christ our Lord" (Romans 1:1–4). (Because this passage was not understood in the context of messianic enthronement, it led to the heresy of Adoptionism which maintained that Jesus was not divine but a human being "adopted" as his son by the Father.)

But Mary, the new Eve and the mother of the Messiah does not exhaust the meaning of this figure. She is prefigured by the virgin daughter Israel, Yahweh's spouse.

> For your Maker is your husband,
> > the LORD of hosts is his name;
> the Holy One of Israel is your Redeemer,
> > the God of the whole earth he is called. (Isaiah 54:5)

> Writhe and groan, O daughter Zion,
> > like a woman in labor. (Micah 4:10)

But the analogy is not always a flattering one. Hosea had used his own tragic love life as a lesson for Israel, God's bride. But Isaiah continues the analogy in a bitter condemnation:

> But as for you, come here,
>> you children of a sorceress,
>> you offspring of an adulterer and a whore.
> Whom are you mocking?
>> Against whom do you open your mouth wide
>> and stick out your tongue?
> Are you not children of transgression,
>> the offspring of deceit— (Isaiah 57:3–4)

But his mercy endures forever, and so Jeremiah could promise:

> The days are surely coming, says the LORD, when I will make a new covenant with the house of Israel and the house of Judah. It will not be like the covenant that I made with their ancestors when I took them by the hand to bring them out of the land of Egypt—a covenant that they broke, *though I was their husband, says the LORD*. But this is the covenant that I will make with the house of Israel after those days, says the LORD: I will put my law within them, and I will write it on their hearts; and I will be their God, and they shall be my people. (Jeremiah 31:31–34) [emphasis added]

And finally, does not the woman clothed with the sun, moon and stars speak to us of Holy Mother Church? She is the mother not only of the Messiah, but also her other children: "Then the dragon was angry with the woman, and went off to make war on the rest of her children, those who keep the commandments of God and hold the testimony of Jesus" (12:17).

Also the early members of the church thought of themselves as the New Israel. "For neither circumcision nor uncircumcision is anything; but a new creation is everything! As for those who will follow is rule—peace be upon them, and mercy, and upon the Israel of God" (Galatians 6:15–16).

Just as Israel of old experienced God's salvation fleeing from Pharaoh to the safety of the desert, so the New Israel, fleeing from the Roman emperor, finds God's salvation symbolized by the desert.

REFLECTION

Mary, A Sign of Sure Hope and Solace for God's People in Pilgrimage.

In the bodily and spiritual glory which she possesses in heaven, the Mother of Jesus continues in this present world as the image and first flowering of the Church as she is to be perfected in the world to come. Likewise, Mary shines forth on earth, until the day of the Lord shall come (cf. 2 Pet 3:10) as a sign of sure hope and solace for the pilgrim People of God.... Let the entire body of the faithful pour forth persevering prayer to the Mother of God and Mother of his people. Let them implore that she who aided the beginnings of the Church by her prayers may now, exalted as she is in heaven, above all the saints and angels intercede with her Son in the fellowship of all the saints. May she do so until all the peoples of the human family, whether they are honored with the name of Christian or whether they still do not know their Saviour, are happily gathered together in peace and harmony into the one People of God. (*Lumen gentium,* 68)

CHAPTER TWENTY-EIGHT

THE MOTHER OF ALL WARS (12:7–12)

And war broke out in heaven; Michael and his angels fought against the dragon. The dragon and his angels fought back, but they were defeated, and there was no longer any place for them in heaven. The great dragon was thrown down, that ancient serpent, who is called the Devil and Satan, the deceiver of the whole world—he was thrown down to the earth, and his angels were thrown down with him.

> Then I heard a loud voice in heaven, proclaiming,
> "Now have come the salvation and the power
> > and the kingdom of our God
> > and the authority of his Messiah,
> for the accuser of our comrades has been thrown down,
> > who accuses them day and night before our God.
> But they have conquered him by the blood of the Lamb
> > and by the word of their testimony,
> for they did not cling to life even in the face of death.
> Rejoice then, you heavens
> > and those who dwell in them!
> But woe to the earth and the sea,
> > for the devil has come down to you
> with great wrath,
> > because he knows that his time is short!"

As we are being swept up to view the mother of all wars being waged in heaven, we should not forget the beleaguered, confused, despairing community on earth for whom this book was written. Theirs is not a fair battle. As surely as the power of Light is triumphing in Heaven, just as surely does the power of darkness seem to be triumphing on earth. It seems that the powers of darkness have the upper hand, unlike the prototype war in heaven. The members of the community need this heavenly vision to give them hope in their own struggle.

But it should be remembered that the vision of the war in heaven is not a preview of coming attractions. It is a memory that gives them hope. There is the assurance in the prologue of Saint John: "The light shines in the darkness, and the darkness did not overcome it"(1:5). Whatever power Satan may have had, he's had a bad fall from which he will never recover. We can take that on the word of Jesus: "The seventy returned with joy, saying, 'Lord, in your name even the demons submit to us!' He said to them, 'I watched Satan fall from heaven like a flash of lightning'" (Luke 10:17–18).

The same victory is reaffirmed in John's Gospel. "Now is the judgment of this world; now the ruler of this world will be driven out" (John 12:31). The hour of Jesus is the last hour of Satan. His futile gasp was in the feeble effort to take control of the "hour." "Then Satan entered into Judas called Iscariot, who was one of the twelve; he went away and conferred with the chief priests and officers of the temple police about how he might betray him to them" (Luke 22:3). But Satan was powerless, capable only of little skirmishes.

"For this reason the Father loves me, because I lay down my life in order to take it up again. No one takes it from me, but I lay it down of my own accord. I have power to lay it down, and I have power to take it up again. I have received this command from my Father" (John 10:17–18). The battle is over. Jesus is Lord!

That does not mean, of course, that we can let down our guard totally. The forces of evil will continue to make their last desperate stand. But we know for certain that, with Jesus, we are on the winning side and we don't have to harbor an anxiety bordering on despair.

> What then are we to say about these things? If God is for us, who is against us? He who did not withhold his own Son, but gave him up for all of us, will he not with him also give us everything else? Who will bring any charge against God's elect? It is God who justifies. Who is to condemn? It is Christ Jesus, who died, yes, who

was raised, who is at the right hand of God, who indeed intercedes for us. Who will separate us from the love of Christ? Will
hardship, or distress, or persecution, or famine, or nakedness, or
peril, or sword? As it is written,

> "For your sake we are being killed all day long;
>   we are accounted as sheep to be slaughtered."

No, in all these things we are more than conquerors through him
who loved us. For I am convinced that neither death, nor life, nor
angels, nor rulers, nor things present, nor things to come, nor
powers, nor height, nor depth, nor anything else in all creation,
will be able to separate us from the love of God in Christ Jesus our
Lord. (Romans 8:36–39)

REFLECTION

At the Lamb's high feast we sing,
Praise to our victorious King,
Who has washed us in the tide
Flowing from his wounded side;
Praise we Christ whose love divine,
Gives his sacred blood for wine,
Gives his body for the feast,
Christ the victim, Christ the Priest.
Where the paschal blood is poured,
Death's dark angel sheathes the sword;
Israel's hosts triumphant go
through the wave that drowns the foe.
Praise we Christ whose blood was shed,
Paschal victim, Paschal bread;
With sincerity and love, Eat we manna from above.
Mighty victim from the sky,
Hell's fierce powers beneath you lie.
You have conquered in the fight,
You have brought us life and light;

Now no more can death appall
Now no more the grave enthrall;
You have opened Paradise,
and in you the Saints shall rise.
(Translated from the Latin by Robert Campbell [1814–1868])

CHAPTER TWENTY-NINE

ANOTHER VIEW OF CREATION (13:1–4)

Then the dragon took his stand on the sand of the seashore. And I saw a beast rising out of the sea, having ten horns and seven heads; and on its horns were ten diadems, and on its heads were blasphemous names. And the beast that I saw was like a leopard, its feet were like a bear's, and its mouth was like a lion's mouth. And the dragon gave it his power and his throne and great authority. One of its heads seemed to have received a death-blow, but its mortal wound had been healed. In amazement the whole earth followed the beast. They worshiped the dragon, for he had given his authority to the beast, and they worshiped the beast, saying, "Who is like the beast, and who can fight against it?"

Satan, a figure that emerges in the Biblical text after the Babylonian exile, under the influence of Persian dualistic Manichaeism, has several job descriptions. He is the prosecuting attorney in the great trial of God's people (Revelation12:10) as he was in the Book of Job. Later on he becomes the "Father of Lies" and the personification of the forces of evil who tries to increase his following by seducing people away from God. In this role, his weapons are dishonesty and temptation, which he even brought to bear on God's Son, the Messiah (Matthew 4).

When his seductive lying fails, he resorts to violence and becomes the commander in chief in the war against God's people and the very personification of the powers of evil, chaos and mayhem. Thus he is perceived as the figure who would return the beauty and order and goodness of God's creation back into chaos.

To understand this we must realize that the Genesis account of creation is but one of several mythologies (stories which convey deep truths, but are not to be taken at face value) of creation in the Bible. The official teaching of the Catholic church on the seven-day account in Genesis 1 is that it, like everything in the first eleven chapters of Genesis, "relates in simple and figurative language, adapted to the understanding of a less developed people the fundamental truths presupposed for the economy of salvation, as well as the popular description of the human race and of the chosen people" (Pontifical Biblical Commission, 1948).

Recognizing this, we can see how the author of the Book of Revelation uses a mythology of creation that is Biblical but less familiar to us. It is no less God's word of truth than the first chapters of Genesis.

> You crushed the heads of Leviathan;
>> you gave him as food for the creatures of the wilderness.
> You cut openings for springs and torrents;
>> you dried up ever-flowing streams.
> Yours is the day, yours also the night;
>> you established the luminaries and the sun.
> You have fixed all the bounds of the earth;
>> you made summer and winter. (Psalm 74:14–17)

Leviathan is synonymous with chaos, out of which Yahweh brings creation in Genesis. "On that day the Lord with his cruel and great and strong sword will punish Leviathan the fleeing serpent, Leviathan the twisting serpent, and he will kill the dragon that is in the sea" (Isaiah 27:1). Creation is a cosmic battle in which Yahweh triumphs.

> By his power he stilled the Sea;
>> by his understanding he struck down Rahab.
> By his wind the heavens were made fair;
>> his hand pierced the fleeing serpent. (Job 26:12–13)

Yahweh brings about the goodness of creation by overpowering the serpent, Rahab, alias Leviathan.

> . . .
> who is as mighty as you, O LORD?
> Your faithfulness surrounds you.
> You rule the raging of the sea;

> when its waves rise, you still them.
> You crushed Rahab like a carcass;
> you scattered your enemies with your mighty arm. (Psalm 89:8–10)

> Awake, awake, put on strength,
> O arm of the LORD!
> Awake, as in days of old,
> the generations of long ago!
> Was it not you who cut Rahab in pieces,
> who pierced the dragon?
> Was it not you who dried up the sea,
> the waters of the great deep;
> who made the depths of the sea a way
> for the redeemed to cross over? (Isaiah 51:9–10)

The above passage shows that creation was never considered a *fait accompli*. It is an ongoing process. When God brought his people from slavery to freedom in the Passover, this was the continuation of creation. And the Book of Revelation considers that God's saving action in conquering the chaos and evil force that is the Roman Empire is just one more manifestation of his creative activity.

REFLECTION

Still another view of creation is that of Paul, who in his mature theology, sees it neither as a battle nor a seven-day process. It is the Father's eternal plan, centered in his incarnate Son:

> He has rescued us from the power of darkness and transferred us into the kingdom of his beloved Son, in whom we have redemption, the forgiveness of sins.
>
> He is the image of the invisible God, the firstborn of all creation; for in him all things in heaven and on earth were created, things visible and invisible, whether thrones or dominions or rulers or powers—all things have been created through him and for him. He himself is before all things, and in him all things hold

together. He is the head of the body, the church; he is the beginning, the firstborn from the dead, so that he might come to have first place in everything. For in him all the fullness of God was pleased to dwell, and through him God was pleased to reconcile to himself all things, whether on earth or in heaven, by making peace through the blood of his cross. (Colossians 1:13–20)

CHAPTER THIRTY

DETERMINISM (13:5–10)

The beast was given a mouth uttering haughty and blasphemous words, and it was allowed to exercise authority for forty-two months. It opened its mouth to utter blasphemies against God, blaspheming his name and his dwelling, that is, those who dwell in heaven. Also it was allowed to make war on the saints and to conquer them. It was given authority over every tribe and people and language and nation, and all the inhabitants of the earth will worship it, everyone whose name has not been written from the foundation of the world in the book of life of the Lamb that was slaughtered.

> Let anyone who has an ear listen:
> If you are to be taken captive,
>> into captivity you go;
> if you kill with the sword,
>> with the sword you must be killed.
> Here is a call for the endurance and faith of the saints.

According to an Old Testament view of history, God was in such complete control that his enemies were powerless. Even the Egyptian god, Pharaoh, could not make a move or decision on his own, for God hardened his heart (Exodus 7:3).

Notice the similar language of this passage: "The beast *was given a mouth... was allowed to make war and to conquer... was given authority.*" In such a situation, the devil doesn't have a snowball's chance in hell! Mortals do not fare much better. Some were lucky enough to get their names written in the book of life, through no merit of their own. Some were predestined for captivity, and there is nothing they can do about it.

All of this, of course, flows from the point of view that if it happened, God caused it to happen. Human choice, and hence guilt, does not come into play. We must constantly remember that this is a primitive way of looking at history. It can sometimes be misleading, if not dangerous. It easily happens that one confuses the events of history with God's activity in history.

The most prominent example of this in the Old Testament was the *ban* or in Hebrew, *herem*. It was a defense mechanism, used by the peoples of the ancient world, not just the Hebrews. It flowed from a policy of total non-tolerance. To preserve one's own values, one eradicated the values of surrounding peoples lest they be a threat to one's own. And the only way to get rid of their values was to annihilate them. It was not unlike weeding a vegetable garden where no distinction was made between destructive weeds and wild flowers. All are ripped out in order that the vegetables might survive.

> Take care not to make a covenant with the inhabitants of the land to which you are going, or it will become a snare among you. You shall tear down their altars, break their pillars, and cut down their sacred poles (for you shall worship no other god, because the Lord, whose name is Jealous, is a jealous God). You shall not make a covenant with the inhabitants of the land, for when they prostitute themselves to their gods and sacrifice to their gods, someone among them will invite you, and you will eat of the sacrifice. And you will take wives from among their daughters for your sons, and their daughters who prostitute themselves to their gods will make your sons also prostitute themselves to their gods. (Exodus 34:12–16)

That this was the practice of all nations and not just Israel is shown from Deuteronomy 28:47–57. It was not a question of cruelty, but of survival. It was Israel alone, however, that then attributed this survival tactic to the will of God. And that is a very primitive and naïve attitude easily slipping into moral self-righteousness: "Since we are God's people, and we did it, it must have been God's will." Much cruelty and suffering throughout history have been wrought by those who attributed their atrocities to God's will. They measured God's will by what they did, rather than seeking God's will and doing it.

Even the Crusaders, as they killed the non–Roman Catholic population of Jerusalem, and then in the fourth Crusade committed unspeakable abominations against Constantinople and its Orthodox population, cried out *Deus lo Vult.* (God wills it!) Despite what some may believe, radical Muslims were not the first to canonize terrorism!

As much as we might characterize the outrages of history as misguided and wrong, have we advanced much when we dropped the atomic bomb on innocent civilian populations? We put them to the *ban,* obliterating them and everything about them, claiming that it was justified, and the moral and ethical thing to do. The reason, of course, was our belief that God was on our side!

Inspiration affirms that a writing is the word of God. That does not mean that God corrected the human author's spelling, improved his vocabulary or rectified his grammar. Nor does it mean that God "spiritualized" the primitive attitudes that were part of a primitive mentality of an emerging people. It is an error to read a Western mentality into the Old Testament or to expect a more highly developed morality from the Book of Revelation, which was so heavily influenced by the Old Testament. God accepted the Israelite's as they were, and so should we.

In reading the Bible, we must realize (without denying it is the Word of God), the human element with its human limitations sometimes takes center stage. God did not take pen or word processor in his hand. It was a human author who wrote it all down. Everything that the inspired human author attributes to God, as the old song says, "ain't necessarily so!"

Too often, religious people tend to presume that what they do is God's will. Modesty and humility require that we continually seek the will of God and do it.

REFLECTION

When you pray, pray like this: our father, who art in heaven, hallowed be thy name, thy kingdom come, thy will be done on earth as it is in heaven.

He came out and went, as was his custom to the Mount of Olives; and the disciples followed him. When he reached the place, he said to them, "Pray that you may not come into the time of trial." Then he withdrew from them about a stone's throw, knelt down, and prayed, "Father, if you are willing, remove this cup from me; yet, not my will but yours be done." (Luke 22:39–42)

CHAPTER THIRTY-ONE

IDOL WORSHIP (13:11–15)

Then I saw another beast that rose out of the earth; it had two horns like a lamb and it spoke like a dragon. It exercises all the authority of the first beast on its behalf, and it makes the earth and its inhabitants worship the first beast, whose mortal wound had been healed. It performs great signs, even making fire come down from heaven to earth in the sight of all; and by the signs that it is allowed to perform on behalf of the beast, it deceives the inhabitants of earth, telling them to make an image for the beast that had been wounded by the sword and yet lived; and it was allowed to give breath to the image of the beast so that the image of the beast could even speak and cause those who would not worship the image of the beast to be killed.

We are made in the image and likeness of God. Idols are gods made in the image of ourselves and the likeness of our needs. The human race was created out of nothing, and when we form our gods out of nothing that is exactly what they are: nothing. During the Babylonian exile (587–537 B.C.) the prophet known as Deutero-Isaiah describes them by having God question them:

Tell us what is to come hereafter,
    that we may know that you are gods;
do good, or do harm,
    that we may be afraid and terrified.
You, indeed, are nothing
    and your work is nothing at all;
    whoever chooses you is an abomination. (Isaiah 41:23–24)

To whom will you liken me and make me equal,
    and compare me, as though we were alike

Those who lavish gold from the purse,
and weigh out silver in the scales—
they hire a goldsmith, who makes it into a god;
then they fall down and worship!
They lift it to their shoulders, they carry it,
they set it in its place, and it stands there;
it cannot move from its place.
If one cries out to it, it does not answer
or save anyone from trouble. (Isaiah 46:5–7)

However, several centuries later the power of the Roman Empire was brought to bear so that by trickery and machination, the idols appeared to have the power of doing "wonders" and "answering" questions. But one would be hard put to say God has done this, or "this is the word of the Lord." One could say "Houdini has done this" or "This is the word of a charlatan." But that would be a deceptive religious game, that provides no help in a crisis. Whether they were the mute idols of the Babylonian Exile or the ventriloquist's idols of the time of the Book of Revelation, there was no contest when they were compared with the Lord! He alone could work wonders and speak his word.

The charlatan idol referred to here is of the Emperor Nero, who, after having been impeached by the Roman senate for high crimes and misdemeanors, either dispatched himself with a sword or had a servant do it. The circumstances of his death were so cloudy that the rumor arose that he would rise again! He was so despised and evil that when any tragedy occurred, it was reputed to be the work of *"Nero Redivivus,"* like a horror movie sequel. The deceptive idols of him set up during the reign of Domitian, thirty years after Nero's death, reinforced the legend.

Domitian was the first beast who gave life to Nero, the second beast, a clone of his predecessor. Domitian was so despised for his capricious and chaotic torture and persecution that the plot to overthrow and assassinate him was led by his wife!

Yet, no matter how the inspired author of both the Old and New Testaments may mock idols and proclaim their nothingness, their worshipers are not aware of that. For them the idol stands for something, whether it is glory, power, riches or sex, to name just a few possibilities. Idol worshipers are not stupid or ignorant. They have needs, and they think they can be satisfied by the real or imaginary power that stands behind the idol. No one is immune to idol worship, since no one is immune to sin, including the church.

REFLECTION

The church is an evangelizer, but she begins by being evangelized herself. She is the community of believers, the community of hope, lived and communicated, the community of brotherly love, and she needs to listen unceasingly to what she must believe, to her reasons for hoping, to the new commandment of love. She is the People of God immersed in the world, and often tempted by idols, and she always needs to hear the proclamation of the 'mighty works of God' which converted her to the Lord; she always needs to be called afresh by Him and reunited. In brief, this means she has a constant need of being evangelized if she wishes to retain freshness, vigor and strength in order to proclaim the Gospel. The Second Vatican Council recalled and the 1974 Synod vigorously took up this theme of the Church which is evangelized by constant conversion and renewal in order to evangelize the world with credibility. (Paul VI "On Evangelization")

CHAPTER THIRTY-TWO

"SIX-SIX-SIX" (13:16–18)

Also it causes all, both small and great, both rich and poor, both free and slave, to be marked on the right hand or the forehead, so that no one can buy or sell who does not have the mark, that is, the name of the beast or the number of its name. This calls for wisdom: let anyone with understanding calculate the number of the beast, for it is the number of a person. Its number is six hundred sixty-six.

In the nineteen hundred years since the author wrote this passage, almost every generation has had its own candidate for 666. Most recently Osama bin Laden, architect of the 9/11 terrorist attack on the United States, has been labeled with the number. A seminarian working as an orderly in a hospital in the U.S. Bible Belt was asked by a nurse to resolve a debate that she and another nurse were having. "Didn't the pope wear that tall head-dress to hide 666 on his forehead?" When he replied in the negative, she assured her coworker that it was no doubt on his belt buckle! The pope has been the prime 666 choice of anti-Catholics for generations.

However, Genghis Khan, Mohammed, Saladin (who defeated the crusaders), Luther, the superior general of the Jesuits, Hitler and Stalin have all been nominated as candidates. However, this is not a quiz show or a guessing game. The author had a specific person in mind. He fully expected that his readers, "with understanding" would be able to identify the beast. It might take a little "wisdom," but he was confident that those who received this document at the end of the first century would know exactly whom he had in mind. He expected this because the Christian communities of Asia Minor knew his code. They had no number system. Whether they spoke Aramaic, Greek or Latin (Hebrew was already a dead language), they did not count with numbers. The letters of the alphabet took their place: A = 1; B = 2; C = 3, etc. Check out the cornerstone of any public building and you will get the picture. The date is given as letters of the Latin alphabets, hence they are called roman numerals.

The same holds for Aramaic, the author's original language, and Greek, the language in which he is writing. This situation makes it convenient to communicate in numbers that are code for a word. The practice was common in the ancient world and is called *gematria*. That some members of the Christian community were familiar with it is evident from Matthew's genealogy of Jesus. He omits some names in order to have 14–14–14. In *gematria,* 14 is also written 4–6–4. Those are the letters DVD and everyone knew whose name that was! Matthew's genealogy uses fourteen three times, to show that Jesus is the new David—not squared, but cubed!

The number 666 in Aramaic is the code for Nero Caesar, one of the cruelest and most capricious tyrants history has produced. A recent archaeological discovery shows that he set up a temple to himself in Greece. He enrolled himself among the gods in the Roman pantheon, and citizens were expected to show their loyalty to the Empire by the appropriate worship. When it was accomplished, they received a mark or sign showing that they had exercised their civic duty and were roman citizens in good standing. But for Christians, it was a denial of the Lordship of Jesus Christ.

REFLECTION

I therefore, the prisoner in the Lord, beg you to lead a life worthy of the calling to which you have been called, with all humility and gentleness, with patience, bearing with one another in love, making every effort to maintain the unity of the Spirit in the bond of peace. There is one body and one Spirit, just as you were called to the one hope of your calling, one Lord, one faith, one baptism, one God and Father of all, who is above all and through all and in all. (Ephesians 4:1–6)

CHAPTER THIRTY-THREE

"IS IT I, LORD?" (13:16–18)

The identification of 666, while referring first of all to Nero, may also have another designation, namely, you and me.

The title for Jesus in the Book of Revelation is "Lord of lords and King of kings" (17:14 and 19:16). The numerical equivalent in Aramaic is 777. While indeed 666 can be said to be the numerical equivalent of Nero Caesar, nevertheless, following the author's penchant for having more than one meaning for the same symbol, 666 can also apply to anyone who tries to usurp the lordship of Jesus. Such impostors and usurpers come close to 777, the perfect number of the Lord of lords and King of kings, but fall short.

They are frauds, phonies and charlatans. Thus, those who point the finger at the tyrants and despots of history as personifications of 666 are on the right track. The early Christian community had already identified some of them with a variety of titles:

"As to the coming of our Lord Jesus Christ and our being gathered together to him, [the Greek also means "caught up" or "raptured"] we beg you, brothers and sisters, not to be quickly shaken in mind or alarmed, either by spirit or by word or by letter, as though from us, to the effect that the day of the Lord is already here. Let no one deceive you in any way; for that day will not come unless the rebellion comes first and *the lawless one* is revealed, the one destined for destruction. He opposes and exalts himself above every so-called god or object of worship, so that he takes his seat in the temple of God, declaring himself to be God" (2 Thessalonians 1:1–4). The author has in mind the repetition of the enthronement of the Abomination of the Desolation, King Antiochus Epiphanes, in the Jerusalem Temple in 167 B.C.

"And if anyone says to you at that time, 'Look! Here is the Messiah!' or 'Look! There he is!'—do not believe it. *False messiahs and false prophets* will appear and produce signs and omens, to lead astray, if possible, the elect" (Mark 13:21–22)[emphasis added].

Children, it is the last hour! As you have heard that *antichrist* is coming, so now *many antichrists* have come. From this we know that it is the last hour. They went out from us, but they did not belong to us; for if they had belonged to us, they would have remained with us. But by going out they made it plain that none of them belongs to us. But you have been anointed by the Holy One, and all of you have knowledge. I write to you, not because you do not know the truth, but because you know it, and you know that no lie comes from the truth. Who is the liar but the one who denies that Jesus is the Christ. This is *the antichrist*, the one who denies the Father and the Son. No one who denies the Son has the Father; everyone who confesses the Son has the Father also. Let what you heard from the beginning abide in you....(1 John 2:18–24a)[emphasis added]

Beloved, do not believe every spirit, but test the spirits to see whether they are from God; for many false prophets have gone out into the world. By this you know the Spirit of God: every spirit that confesses that Jesus Christ has come in the flesh is from God, and every spirit that does not confess Jesus is not from God. And this is the spirit of *the antichrist*, of which you have heard that it is coming; and now it is already in the world. (1 John 4:1–3)[emphasis added]

Many deceivers have gone out into the world, those who do not confess that Jesus Christ has come in the flesh; any such person is *the deceiver and the antichrist!* (2 John 7)[emphasis added]

In the Book of Revelation the title *antichrist* is not found. Nor is it found in the letters of Paul or any of the Gospels. It is found only in the Johannine Epistles, and there it refers not to the vicious, persecuting enemy from without, but the "heretic" from within who, denying Jesus' humanity, has departed from the fellowship of the believers.

It is obvious that the opponents of Christ were to be found under many guises. The early Christians even felt comfortable in designating some of their errant fellow Christians as antichrists. Some later Christians, especially television evangelists, have broadened the designation to apply to everyone they don't like. Perhaps they are not far off the mark, except that they do not include themselves!

Are not all of us antichrists and deserving to be marked with 666, to the extent that we are sinners? To sin is to oppose the lordship of Jesus. Paul found that some of the faithful at Corinth had even become idolaters of the charisms or spiritual gifts. He reminded them:

> Now concerning spiritual gifts, brothers and sisters, I do not want you to be uninformed. You know that when you were pagans, you were enticed and led astray to idols that could not speak. Therefore I want you to understand that no one speaking by the Spirit of God ever says "Let Jesus be cursed!" and no one can say "Jesus is Lord" except by the Holy Spirit. (1 Corinthians 12:1–3)

REFLECTION

> If we say that we have fellowship with God while we are walking in darkness, we lie and do not do what is true, but if we walk in the light as he himself is in the light, we have fellowship with one another, and the blood of Jesus his Son cleanses us from all sin. If we say that we have no sin, we deceive ourselves, and the truth is not in us. If we confess our sins, he who is faithful and just will forgive us our sins and cleanse us from all unrighteousness. If we say that we have not sinned, we make him a liar, and his word is not in us. (1 John 1:6–10)

CHAPTER THIRTY-FOUR

THE SEXUAL REVOLUTION (14:1–5)

Then I looked, and there was the Lamb, standing on Mount Zion! And with him were one hundred forty-four thousand who had his name and his Father's name written on their foreheads. And I heard a voice from heaven like the sound of many waters and like the sound of loud thunder; the voice I heard was like the sound of harpists playing on their harps, and they sing a new song before the throne and before the four living creatures and before the elders. No one could learn that song except the one hundred forty-four thousand who have been redeemed from the earth. It is these who have not defiled themselves with women, for they are virgins; these follow the Lamb wherever he goes. They have been redeemed from humankind as first fruits for God and the Lamb, and in their mouth no lie was found; they are blameless.

No symbol of the Book of Revelation should be taken at its face value. The lamb was not a lamb; it was Jesus. The number 144,000 was not 12 times 12 times 1000, it was a vast, uncountable number. And the virgins are not virgins because they have not had sexual intercourse. They are the ones who are not branded with 666, the name of the beast. They are branded with the name of Jesus and his Father ("who had his name and his Father's name written on their foreheads"). The author is not talking about their celibacy, but their fidelity. He uses the imagery of sex to reinforce that "in their mouth no lie was found; they are blameless."

"For all the nations have drunk of the wine of the wrath of her fornication, and the kings of the earth have committed fornication with her....And the kings of the earth, who committed fornication and lived in luxury with her, will weep and wail over her when they see the smoke of her burning" (cf. 18:3, 9). The author takes his cue, as he so often does, from the Old Testament. There, the worst sin that the Israelites committed was "fornicating with the gods of the gentiles." In Genesis 2—3 the very story of the "original sin" by our first parents is called by the Pontifical Biblical Commission an account "in simple and figurative language, adapted to the understanding of a less developed people, the fundamental truths presupposed for the economy of salvation, as well as the *popular description* of the origin of the human race and of the Chosen people" (letter from the Pontifical Biblical Commission to Cardinal Suhard, 1948).

The author of the story of the Fall writes what is called an etiological account. He looks for the *aetios,* or cause, of the predominant sin that he sees around him. It is infidelity to the covenant with Yahweh by using one's sexuality to obtain fertility in the sexual rituals of the god and goddess of fertility, Baal and Astarte.

> And it shall be like people, like priest;
> > I will punish them for their ways,
> > and repay them for their deeds.
> They shall eat, but not be satisfied;
> > they shall play the whore, but not multiply;
> because they have forsaken the LORD
> > to devote themselves to whoredom.
>
> . . .
>
> For a spirit of whoredom has led them astray,
> > and they have played the whore, forsaking their God.
> They sacrifice on the tops of the mountains,
> > and make offerings upon the hills. (Hosea 4:9–13)

The prophet knows whereof he speaks. He lived in an age when fornication with the cultic prostitutes was seen as the way to attain fertility. His contemporaries wrote off Yahweh as a specialist in transportation out of Egypt. They went to other specialists, like Baal and his wife Astarte, to assure fertility. That was their specialization and their cultic prostitutes on the "high places" were the means to attain that fertility.

God will not be mocked. He told Hosea, whose wife had become one of the cultic prostitutes, to name one of his children: *Lo-Ami,* (not my people).

That is the opposite of the covenant formula: "I will be your God and you will be my people." Both the prophet's own tragic love life and his children were to be signs of how Israel was treating its God.

It is no surprise then, that the author of Revelation identifies infidelity and idolatry with their expression in the Old Testament. Four times in chapter 17, and in 19:2, the author identifies the whore who brought about fornication. (Babylon is his code name for Rome).

> Then one of the seven angels who had the seven bowls came and said to me, "Come, I will show you the judgment of the great whore who is seated on many waters, with whom the kings of the earth have committed fornication, and with the wine of whose fornication the inhabitants of the earth have become drunk." So he carried me away in the spirit into a wilderness, and I saw a woman sitting on a scarlet beast that was full of blasphemous names, and it had seven heads and ten horns. The woman was clothed in purple and scarlet, and adorned with gold and jewels and pearls, holding in her hand a golden cup full of abominations and the impurities of her fornication; and on her forehead was written a name, a mystery: "Babylon the great, mother of whores and of earth's abominations." And I saw that the woman was drunk with the blood of the saints and the blood of the witnesses to Jesus. (17:1–6)

> After this I heard what seemed to be the loud voice of a great multitude in heaven, saying,
> "Hallelujah!
> Salvation and glory and power to our God,
>   for his judgments are true and just;
> he has judged the great whore
>   who corrupted the earth with her fornication,
> and he has avenged on her the blood of his servants. (19:1–2)

REFLECTION

Living at a time that is called the sexual revolution, when all too frequently sex has lost its meaning as an expression of love, and the pleasure derived from sex is an end in itself, it is good to hear the words of the prophets. They remind us that sexual intimacy is a sign of our intimacy with God, and sexual infidelity is a sign of disloyalty to the God who loves us.

The American bishops carried the analogy into the liturgy in a startling and marvelous affirmation:

> We are Christians because through the Christian Community, we have met Jesus Christ, heard his word of invitation and responded to him in faith. We assemble together at Mass in order to speak our faith over again in community and by speaking it to renew and deepen it....People in love make signs of love and celebrate their love for the dual purpose of expressing and deepening that love. We too, must express in signs, our love for Christ and each other. (*Statement on Music in the Liturgy*, 1968)

CHAPTER THIRTY-FIVE

WHAT TIME IS IT? (14:6–8)

Then I saw another angel flying in midheaven, with an eternal
gospel to proclaim to those who live on the earth—to every
nation and tribe and language and people. He said in a loud
voice, "Fear God and give him glory, for the hour of his judgment
has come; and worship him who made heaven and earth, the sea
and the springs of water.

Then another angel, a second, followed, saying, "Fallen,
fallen is Babylon the great! She has made all nations drink of the
wine of the wrath of her fornication."

The author is quite comfortable moving from the past to the present to the
future, and none of the tenses of the verbs is to be taken at face value. They
are not designations of time as found on a calendar, but in God's point of
view. God is eternal, as is his plan, and in a very real sense to speak of past,
present and future is to calculate them from our point of view, not God's.
In him is only the eternal now.

That is why the author can speak of the hour of the final judgment as
having come, when according to our reckoning it is still in the future. He
also speaks of Babylon (read Roman Empire) as having fallen, when, as we
know from our perspective, it still had a few more centuries to go, and
unbeknownst to the author, became Christian before it collapsed.

In the infant church, apocalyptic time-keeping was confusing even to
the early Christians. With some, when the future coming of Christ did not
become a present event for them, they forgot that they were dealing with
an apocalyptic clock, and began to think that they had been deceived. The
author of the second letter of Peter, which is believed to have been written
even later than the Apocalypse, had to remind them that they had to shift
gears and get on to God's time: "But do not ignore this one fact, beloved,
that with the Lord one day is like a thousand years, and a thousand years

are like one day. The Lord is not slow about his promise, as some think of slowness, but is patient with you" (2 Peter 3:8–9).

REFLECTION

Greek has two words for time: *kairos* and *chronos*. The latter is the preferred word of the Greek thinkers who perceived time as just going round and round in an endless repetitive cycle. "What goes around comes around" expresses that attitude. It is time that is dull, boring and predictable. It lies heavy on the hands. Christians, however, preferred the word *kairos*. It is time that is filled with opportunity, pregnant with possibility. It is a time of grace. It is sacramental. It has a goal. God's eternal plan, the mystery hidden from all eternity and centered in Christ is, at every instant, a *kairos*.

> As we work together with him [Christ] we urge you also not to accept the grace of God in vain. For he says,
>
> > "At an acceptable time I have listened to you,
> > and on a day of salvation I have helped you."
>
> See, now is the acceptable time; see, now is the day of salvation! (2 Corinthians 6:1–2)
>
> Besides this, you know what time it is, how it is now the moment for you to wake from sleep. For salvation is nearer to us now than when we became believers; the night is far gone, the day is near. Let us then lay aside the works of darkness and put on the armor of light. (Romans 13:11–12)
>
> But when the fullness of time had come, God sent his Son, born of a woman, born under the law, in order to redeem those who were under the law, so that we might receive adoption as children. And because you are children, God has sent the Spirit of his Son into our hearts, crying, "Abba! Father!" So you are no longer a slave but a child, and if a child then also an heir, through God. (Galatians 4:4–7)

[The Father] chose us in Christ before the foundation of the world to be holy and blameless before him in love. He destined us for adoption as his children through Jesus Christ, according to the good pleasure of his will, to the praise of his glorious grace that he freely bestowed on us in the Beloved. In him we have redemption through his blood, the forgiveness of our trespasses, according to the riches of his grace that he lavished on us. With all wisdom and insight he has made known to us the mystery of his will, according to his good pleasure that he set forth in Christ, as a plan for the fullness of time, to gather up all things in him, things in heaven and things on earth. (Ephesians 1:4–10)

CHAPTER THIRTY-SIX

"GO TO HELL" (14:9–13)

Then another angel, a third, followed them, crying with a loud voice, "Those who worship the beast and its image, and receive a mark on their foreheads or on their hands, they will also drink the wine of God's wrath, poured unmixed into the cup of his anger, and they will be tormented with fire and sulfur in the presence of the holy angels and in the presence of the Lamb. And the smoke of their torment goes up forever and ever. There is no rest day or night for those who worship the beast and its image and for anyone who receives the mark of its name."

Here is a call for the endurance of the saints, those who keep the commandments of God and hold fast to the faith of Jesus.

And I heard a voice from heaven saying, "Write this: Blessed are the dead who from now on die in the Lord." "Yes," says the Spirit, "they will rest from their labors, for their deeds follow them."

While the frightening description of what awaits those who are unfaithful and idolaters rivets our attention with its shocking symbolism, the point should not be missed that the church itself has never declared anyone to be damned, much less condemned anyone to hell, not even Judas. For his own purposes, the author uses his imagination to depict eternal punishment.

Jesus, in Matthew's Gospel, is much more modest, but no less certain in his description: "Then he will say to those at his left hand, 'You that are accursed, depart from me into the eternal fire prepared for the devil and his angels.... 'Truly I tell you, just as you did not do it to one of the least of these, you did not do it to me.' And these will go away into eternal punishment, but the righteous into eternal life" (Matthew 25:41, 45). But even here, the analogy of "eternal fire" is used. And it is analogy, not to be taken literally. Truly, we do not know what either heaven or hell will be like or who will be there.

"What no eye has seen, nor ear heard,
    nor the human heart conceived,
what God has prepared for those who love him"—
these things God has revealed to us through the Spirit; for the Spirit searches everything, even the depths of God. For what human being knows what is truly human except the human spirit that is within? So also no one comprehends what is truly God's except the Spirit of God. (1 Corinthians 2:9–11)

We do know who is in heaven: They are called saints and blessed. The church has assured us that they are with God. We even celebrate a feast for them: All Saints Day. They are the known and unknown ones whose number we hope one day to join.

But blessedly, our knowledge of the inhabitants of hell is nonexistent. And all of the people that we have told to go to hell (in one way or another) may not have found their way. It is good to remember that we are not called to be a judge, for we, too, shall be judged. A story told about Pope Paul VI's birth control commission illustrates the point. A prelate insisted that the church could not change, for if it did what would happen to all those millions who had been condemned to hell for their "offense"? Patty Crowley, a member of the commission from Chicago, said: "Father, do you really believe that God has carried out all of your orders?"

REFLECTION

What I am saying, brothers and sisters, is this: flesh and blood cannot inherit the kingdom of God, nor does the perishable inherit the imperishable. Listen, I will tell you a mystery! We will not all die, but we will all be changed, in a moment, in the twinkling of an eye, at the last trumpet. For the trumpet will sound, and the dead will be raised imperishable, and we will be changed. For this perishable body must put on imperishability, and this mortal body must put on immortality. When this perishable body puts on imperishability, and this mortal body puts on immortality, then the saying that is written will be fulfilled:

> "Death has been swallowed up in victory."
> "Where, O death, is your victory?
>   Where, O death, is your sting?"

The sting of death is sin, and the power of sin is the law. But thanks be to God, who gives us the victory through our Lord Jesus Christ. (1 Corinthians 15:50–57)

CHAPTER THIRTY-SEVEN

THE FINAL JUDGMENT (14:14–20)

Then I looked, and there was a white cloud, and seated on the cloud was one like the Son of Man, with a golden crown on his head, and a sharp sickle in his hand! Another angel came out of the temple, calling with a loud voice to the one who sat on the cloud, "Use your sickle and reap, for the hour to reap has come, because the harvest of the earth is fully ripe." So the one who sat on the cloud swung his sickle over the earth, and the earth was reaped.

Then another angel came out of the temple in heaven, and he too had a sharp sickle. Then another angel came out from the altar, the angel who has authority over fire, and he called with a loud voice to him who had the sharp sickle, "Use your sharp sickle and gather the clusters of the vine of the earth, for its grapes are ripe." So the angel swung his sickle over the earth and gathered the vintage of the earth, and he threw it into the great wine press of the wrath of God. And the wine press was trodden outside the city, and blood flowed from the wine press, as high as a horse's bridle, for a distance of about two hundred miles.

The author is undoubtedly a person of great faith, but also a person of incredible and fantastic imagination. His faith tells him that God will not be mocked. He does not tolerate being toyed with. We may try to play games, but God does not. There will be an end to his patience and it will result in the Last Judgment. In a terribly critical time in the Old Testament, the author of the Book of Daniel said that the Son of Man would mark the time. This was a favorite title of Jesus in the gospels.

"Then they will see 'the Son of Man coming in clouds' with great power and glory. Then he will send out the angels, and gather his elect from the four winds, from the ends of the earth to the ends of heaven"

(Mark 13:26–27). Jesus' description of the Last Judgment-harvest is more modest than that of the author of Revelation.

> When the Son of Man comes in his glory, and all the angels with him, then he will sit on the throne of his glory. All the nations will be gathered before him, and he will separate people one from another as a shepherd separates the sheep from the goats, and he will put the sheep at his right hand and the goats at the left. Then the king will say to those at his right hand, "Come, you that are blessed by my Father, inherit the kingdom prepared for you from the foundation of the world; for I was hungry and you gave me food, I was thirsty and you gave me something to drink, I was a stranger and you welcomed me, I was naked and you gave me clothing, I was sick and you took care of me, I was in prison and you visited me." (Matthew 25:31–36)

And Paul, in his more theological, if not mystical, language says:

> I consider that the sufferings of this present time are not worth comparing with the glory about to be revealed to us. For the creation waits with eager longing for the revealing of the children of God; for the creation was subjected to futility, not of its own will but by the will of the one who subjected it, in hope that the creation itself will be set free from its bondage to decay and will obtain the freedom of the glory of the children of God. We know that the whole creation has been groaning in labor pains until now; and not only the creation, but we ourselves, who have the first-fruits of the Spirit, groan inwardly while we wait for adoption, the redemption of our bodies. For in hope we were saved. Now hope that is seen is not hope. For who hopes for what is seen? But if we hope for what we do not see, we wait for it with patience. (Romans 8:18–25)

REFLECTION

The Second Vatican Council gives another point of view of the end times:

> Let the entire body of the faithful pour forth persevering prayer to the Mother of God and our Mother. Let them implore that she who aided the beginnings of the Church by her prayers, may now, exalted as she is in heaven, above all the saints and angels intercede with her Son in the fellowship of all the saints. May she do so until all the people of the human family, whether they are honored with the name of Christian, or whether they still do not know their saviour are happily gathered together in peace and harmony into the one people of God, for the glory of the most holy and Undivided Trinity. (*Constitution on the Church*, 69)

CHAPTER THIRTY-EIGHT

FEAR OF THE LORD (15:1–4)

Then I saw another portent in heaven, great and amazing: seven angels with seven plagues, which are the last, for with them the wrath of God is ended.

And I saw what appeared to be a sea of glass mixed with fire, and those who had conquered the beast and its image and the number of its name, standing beside the sea of glass with harps of God in their hands. And they sing the song of Moses, the servant of God, and the song of the Lamb:

"Great and amazing are your deeds,
    Lord God the Almighty!
Just and true are your ways,
    King of the nations!
Lord, who will not fear
    and glorify your name
For you alone are holy.
    All nations will come
    and worship before you."

The fear of God can be one of the most self-destructive attitudes that can afflict a person. It is a dreadful thing to spend one's life cringing before a vengeful and angry God. When such an affliction results from reading Scripture, then it has been misread. The word *fear* in the above passage is parallel to *glorify* and is a synonym of it. The fundamental attitude denoted by fear in the Bible is of awe, marvel or amazement—but not cringing in trepidation in the presence of God.

God's Word does not depict an avenger who is out to get us, just waiting for a false move, the god of "ambush spirituality." The oft-quoted bit of wisdom from Proverbs 9:10: "Fear of the Lord is the beginning of wisdom," must be illuminated by the second part of the proverb: "and the knowledge of the Holy One is insight." In the biblical sense, the deepest knowledge is loving union: "And Adam knew his wife Eve."

When God appeared to Moses in the burning bush, he revealed himself not as a God to be feared, but as one who frees and liberates a people bound in slavery and suffering and invites them to himself for a loving embrace. He calls them from the wintertime of bondage and fear of their masters, to the springtime of his love. The Passover is always celebrated as a feast of liberation, rejoicing in the freedom to love. The very name *Yahweh* that he revealed to his people means not just "He is who is" but also "he who is dynamically present to save and cherish."

In Exodus 19:5 Yahweh invites his people to covenant, which is a union of life and love. It has been translated *testament,* and it is so important that we use it to designate the two stages of salvation history, God's plan of love. Paul in Romans 8:15–16 tells us what is the legacy of the Father's testament:

> For you did not receive a spirit of slavery to fall back into fear, but you have received a spirit of adoption. When we cry, "Abba! Father!" it is that very Spirit bearing witness with our spirit that we are children of God, and if children, then heirs, heirs of God and joint heirs with Christ.

And that's quite an inheritance!

We get the proper perspective in 1 John 4:16–19:

> So we have known and believe the love that God has for us.
>
> God is love, and those who abide in love abide in God, and God abides in them. Love has been perfected among us in this: that we may have boldness on the day of judgment, because as he is, so are we in this world. There is no fear in love, but perfect love casts out fear; for fear has to do with punishment, and whoever fears has not reached perfection in love. We love because he first loved us.

No doubt the Old Testament depicts God as a parent, threatening his children if they don't behave. But even parents do that because, like God, they love their children so much. If there is any reason for fear to be part of our spiritual life it comes from an awareness of our own weakness and frailty. That is why Paul gives this advice to the early Christians: "...work out your own salvation with fear and trembling" (Philippians 2:12). In other words, be nervous and fearful, not because you are in the presence of God but because you are aware of your own weakness.

REFLECTION

Do not fear those who kill the body but cannot kill the soul; rather fear him who can destroy both soul and body in hell. Are not two sparrows sold for a penny? Yet not one of them will fall to the ground apart from your Father. And even the hairs of your head are all counted. So do not be afraid; you are of more value than many sparrows. (Matthew 10:28–31)

Peace I leave with you; my peace I give to you. I do not give to you as the world gives. Do not let your hearts be troubled, and do not let them be afraid. (John 14:27)

CHAPTER THIRTY-NINE

CONTROLLING GOD'S TEMPER! (15:5–8)

After this I looked, and the temple of the tent of witness in heaven was opened, and out of the temple came the seven angels with the seven plagues, robed in pure bright linen, with golden sashes across their chests. Then one of the four living creatures gave the seven angels seven golden bowls full of the wrath of God, who lives forever and ever; and the temple was filled with smoke from the glory of God and from his power, and no one could enter the temple until the seven plagues of the seven angels were ended.

In spite of what was said above, for many people the only God they know is the angry God with a volatile temper. He is in the business of wrath. He is watching out for anyone to make a false move, and his overflowing seven (= fullness) bowls of wrath will be tipped over. But God is not in the business either of anger or vengeance. The author depicts him as having the emotion that he himself has (anthropomorphism). It is common for humans to speak of God in an anthropomorphic way but we should never forget the words of Isaiah:

> Seek the LORD while he may be found,
>   call upon him while he is near;
> let the wicked forsake their way,
>   and the unrighteous their thoughts;
> let them return to the LORD, that he may have mercy on them,
>   and to our God, for he will abundantly pardon.
> For my thoughts are not your thoughts,
>   nor are your ways my ways, says the LORD.
> For as the heavens are higher than the earth,
>   so are my ways higher than your ways
>   and my thoughts than your thoughts. (Isaiah 55:6–9)

Or the words of Hosea:

> My heart recoils within me;
>> my compassion grows warm and tender.
> I will not execute my fierce anger;
>> I will not again destroy Ephraim;
> for I am God and no mortal,
>> the Holy One in your midst,
>> and I will not come in wrath. (Hosea 11:8)

Nor should one fall into the previously mentioned (see chapter twenty-three) heresy of Marcion, who asserted that there was a different God for each covenant, one of wrath for the Old Testament and one of compassion for the New Testament. Such a skewed belief can only come from a cursory and superficial reading of the Hebrew Scriptures. It should not be forgotten that when Jesus instructed us to love with our whole heart, mind, soul and strength, he was quoting the only Bible he knew, the Old Testament.

> Hear, O Israel: The LORD is our God, the LORD alone. You shall love the LORD your God with all your heart, and with all your soul, and with all your might. Keep these words that I am commanding you today in your heart. Recite them to your children and talk about them when you are at home and when you are away, when you lie down and when you rise. Bind them as a sign on your hand, fix them as an emblem on your forehead, and write them on the doorposts of your house and on your gates. (Deuteronomy 6:4–9)

Even today for the Jewish people there is always a mezuzah on the doorframe containing this text. It is known as the *Shema* from the first word, *hear,* in Hebrew. And it is the very heart of their faith, often called their creed.

Historically one can understand that sometimes the image of God as having a bad temper has eclipsed the real image of a God filled with love and compassion. When religion becomes preoccupied with law and allows it to eclipse covenant, then God becomes the terrible judge just waiting for us to violate a commandment. He becomes the God of ambush theology. When, however, we return to the deepest meaning of the Bible covenant, we find revealed, even in the thunder and lightning and hellfire and brimstone of Sinai: "The LORD, the LORD, a God merciful and gracious, slow to anger, and abounding in steadfast love and faithfulness."

REFLECTION

One of the most common and frequently used words in the Hebrew Bible is *hesed*, translated "steadfast love."

> So Moses cut two tablets of stone like the former ones; and he rose early in the morning and went up on Mount Sinai, as the LORD [Yahweh] had commanded him, and took in his hand the two tablets of stone. The LORD [Yahweh] descended in the cloud and stood with him there, and proclaimed the name, "The LORD [Yahweh]." The LORD [Yahweh] passed before him, and proclaimed,

> "The LORD [Yahweh], the LORD [Yahweh],
> a God merciful and gracious,
> slow to anger,
> and abounding in steadfast love and faithfulness,
> keeping steadfast love for the thousandth generation,
> forgiving iniquity and transgression and sin,
> yet by no means clearing the guilty." (Exodus 34:4–7)

> Truly the eye of the LORD [Yahweh] is on those who fear him,
> on those who hope in his steadfast love. (Psalm 33:18)

Note: The very name of God, Yahweh, means not just "I am who am," but "I am who am with you to embrace you and save you." Of all the Bible versions only the *New Jerusalem Bible* faithfully uses the sacred name that God revealed to us. The others substitute "LORD" (in Hebrew, *Adonai*) following the Jewish custom.

CHAPTER FORTY

MATURING IN CHRIST (16:1–12)

Then I heard a loud voice from the temple telling the seven angels, "Go and pour out on the earth the seven bowls of the wrath of God."

So the first angel went and poured his bowl on the earth, and a foul and painful sore came on those who had the mark of the beast and who worshiped its image.

The second angel poured his bowl into the sea, and it became like the blood of a corpse, and every living thing in the sea died.

The third angel poured his bowl into the rivers and the springs of water, and they became blood. And I heard the angel of the waters say,

"You are just, O Holy One, who are and were,
    for you have judged these things;
because they shed the blood of saints and prophets,
    you have given them blood to drink.
It is what they deserve!"
And I heard the altar respond,
"Yes, O Lord God, the Almighty,
    your judgments are true and just!"

The fourth angel poured his bowl on the sun, and it was allowed to scorch people with fire; they were scorched by the fierce heat, but they cursed the name of God, who had authority over these plagues, and they did not repent and give him glory.

The fifth angel poured his bowl on the throne of the beast, and its kingdom was plunged into darkness; people gnawed their tongues in agony, and cursed the God of heaven because of their pains and sores, and they did not repent of their deeds.

The sixth angel poured his bowl on the great river Euphrates, and its water was dried up in order to prepare the way for the kings from the east.

We speak of the Old Testament and the New Testament as if there were a clear line of demarcation between them. However, much of the New Testament reflects the struggles, sometimes acrimonious, of the members of the early Christian community to find their identity. They had to determine how much of the "old" would pass over into the new. It was not at all clear how much of the religion that Jesus was born into he intended should endure and become part of the spiritual life of his disciples.

In Matthew's Gospel (28:18–20) he gave his followers the "great commission":

> All authority in heaven and on earth has been given to me. Go therefore and make disciples of all nations, baptizing them in the name of the Father and of the Son and of the Holy Spirit, and teaching them to obey everything that I have commanded you. And remember, I am with you always, to the end of the age.

Notice that new disciples are to be baptized and not circumcised, and they are to obey everything that he commanded, not the law of Moses. Even the great commission, however, is the bottom line that came after a long struggle in Matthew's community.

This struggle of the early Christians to find their identity was a long and painful one. When Paul proclaimed that the Gospel is Jesus and not the law, he was accused by the Jerusalem church of preaching a false gospel (cf. Galatians 1:7), "not that there is another gospel, but there are some who are confusing you and want to pervert the gospel of Christ." Paul thought the issue was so essential to the "Way" of Jesus that: "when Cephas [Peter] came to Antioch, I opposed him to his face" (Galatians 2:11).

While the struggle over the law is well documented, the adaptation by the church of the values of the Old Testament in other areas is less obvious. This passage of the Book of Revelation is a prime example of that struggle. Here, it is not a question of legal observance, but of priorities. Has God called us to hold fast to a covenant of mercy in which the operative word is forgiveness ("Forgive us our trespasses as we forgive those who trespass against us")?

Or has he called us to a life of strict justice, of an eye for an eye, and a tooth for a tooth (a phrase used three times in the Old Testament: Exodus 21:24; Leviticus 24:20; Deuteronomy 19:21). There is no doubt that the moral teaching of Jesus urges us to go beyond tit for tat. The Sermon on the Mount, with its formula of "You have heard that it was said…but I say to you…" shows that the early church members felt they were heirs to a teaching that went beyond that imparted by Moses.

> You have heard that it was said, "An eye for an eye and a tooth for a tooth." But I say to you, Do not resist an evildoer. But if anyone strikes you on the right cheek, turn the other also; and if anyone wants to sue you and take your coat, give your cloak as well; and if anyone forces you to go one mile, go also the second mile. Give to everyone who begs from you, and do not refuse anyone who wants to borrow from you.
>
> You have heard that it was said, "You shall love your neighbor and hate your enemy." But I say to you, love your enemies and pray for those who persecute you, so that you may be children of your Father in heaven; for he makes his sun rise on the evil and on the good, and sends rain on the righteous and on the unrighteous. (Matthew 5:38–45)

Beautiful words! But it was easier for members of the early church to start having a pork roast for Sunday dinner than it was to forgive their enemies. It was a struggle, and the author of Revelation has not yet grown into the maturity of the great challenge of Jesus about mercy and forgiveness.

The seven bowls are filled with "the wrath of God." Then when every body of water is turned to blood, causing the death of every creature in the sea which God had created and called "good," the angel exults: "You are just, O Holy One, who are and were, for you have judged these things; because they shed the blood of saints and prophets, you have given them blood to drink. It is what they deserve!" That is not enough, for even the altar is given a voice in this chorus of vengeance: "And I heard the altar respond, "Yes, O Lord God, the Almighty, your judgments are true and just!"

We may look down on the author who has a long way to go in interiorizing the teaching of Jesus. But so do we, if we really need take a good look at ourselves as well. Our own wars and crimes and atrocities and vengeance and grudges and lack of forgiveness are not corollaries of the Good News of Jesus Christ. Like the author of the Book of Revelation, and the tax collectors and the pagans, we have a long way to go. "For if you love those who love you, what reward do you have? Do not even the tax collectors do the same? And if you greet only your brothers and sisters, what more are you doing than others? Do not even the Gentiles do the same?" (Matthew 5:46–47).

REFLECTION

The quality of mercy is not strain'd,
It droppeth as the gentle rain from heaven
Upon the place beneath: it is twice bless'd;
It blesseth him that gives and him that takes:
'Tis mightiest in the mightiest, it becomes
The throned monarch better than his crown;
His scepter shows the force of temporal power,
The attribute to awe and majesty,
Wherein doth sit the dread and fear of kings;
But mercy is above this scepter'd sway,
It is enthroned in the hearts of kings,
It is an attribute of God himself,
And earthly power doth then show likest God's,
When mercy seasons justice. Therefore, Jew,
Though justice be thy plea, consider this,
That in the course of justice, none of us
Should see Salvation: we do pray for mercy
And that same prayer doth teach us all to render
The deeds of mercy
(Portia to Shylock in the court scene from *The Merchant of Venice*,
Act IV, Scene 1)

CHAPTER FORTY-ONE

THE VOICE OF THE WHISPERING BREEZE (16:13–21)

And I saw three foul spirits like frogs coming from the mouth of the dragon, from the mouth of the beast, and from the mouth of the false prophet. These are demonic spirits, performing signs, who go abroad to the kings of the whole world, to assemble them for battle on the great day of God the Almighty. ("See, I am coming like a thief! Blessed is the one who stays awake and is clothed, not going about naked and exposed to shame.") And they assembled them at the place that in Hebrew is called Harmagedon.

The seventh angel poured his bowl into the air, and a loud voice came out of the temple, from the throne, saying, "It is done!" And there came flashes of lightning, rumblings, peals of thunder, and a violent earthquake, such as had not occurred since people were upon the earth, so violent was that earthquake. The great city was split into three parts, and the cities of the nations fell. God remembered great Babylon and gave her the wine-cup of the fury of his wrath. And every island fled away, and no mountains were to be found; and huge hailstones, each weighing about a hundred pounds, dropped from heaven on people, until they cursed God for the plague of the hail, so fearful was that plague.

The author continues, immersed in his Old Testament mentality and using Old Testament references, to bolster his point of view. Harmagedon is a reference to the plain of Megiddo, with its hill (Har of Megiddo) like a watchtower over the battlefield, which it was.

In his [Josiah's] days Pharaoh Neco king of Egypt went up to the king of Assyria to the river Euphrates. King Josiah went to meet him; but when Pharaoh Neco met him at Megiddo, he killed him. His servants carried him dead in a chariot from Megiddo,

brought him to Jerusalem, and buried him in his own tomb.
(2 Kings 23:28–30)

Megiddo was also called Jezreel and, like Verdun, Pearl Harbor or My Lai in modern history, was so associated with warfare and bloodshed, that it was despised as the symbol of the confidence in the military-industrial complex that replaced faith in Yahweh. The prophet Hosea gave its name to his child as a sign of God's great displeasure with the militarism of Israel.

> When the LORD first spoke through Hosea, the LORD said to Hosea, "Go, take for yourself a wife of whoredom and have children of whoredom, for the land commits great whoredom by forsaking the LORD." So he went and took Gomer daughter of Diblaim, and she conceived and bore him a son.
>
> And the LORD said to him, "Name him Jezreel; for in a little while I will punish the house of Jehu for the blood of Jezreel, and I will put an end to the kingdom of the house of Israel. On that day I will break the bow of Israel in the valley of Jezreel." (Hosea 1:2–5)

There, the author imagines the final battle of the forces of good and evil to take place on the last day. And what a battle! It is cosmic, and really cannot be relegated to any one geographical location or battlefield. Nature itself is involved. The islands that were removed from the scene in chapter six are removed again!

And the mountains also remove themselves from the picture, as an earthquake registering ten on the Richter scale occurs, and hailstones as big as sacks of grain flatten people. And they can still talk! And isn't it amazing that they can curse God? For, in the Bible a curse is a prayer asking God to send evil on someone. This is the first (and last) time that God is asked to bring evil on himself. Strange!

Not really. It is the last conflagration, the final battle. The time could not be more critical. The author is marshaling every possible argument to encourage a beleaguered community, desperate for some sign of hope, in danger of giving up. They are not necessarily concerned with logic or reason. They are seeking dramatic, and what may seem to later generations, bizarre signs of hope. They are engulfed by fantastic chaos and they want fantastic signs that God is in charge. This fantastic passage is for them, and of the very essence of apocalyptic literature, which is neither an essay on evil nor a theological treatise on the power of God, "foul spirits like frogs" and all.

If, after reading this passage, it seems like a nightmare, it should not be forgotten that nightmares are the dreams of the troubled. Apocalyptic literature is for the troubled in troubled times.

REFLECTION

When we are almost stupefied by the incredible catastrophes that the author conjures up to create his vision of the final conflict, it might be good to pause and recall the story of the prophet Elijah in 1 Kings 18:20—19:13. Opposing the syncretism of King Ahab and his wife Jezebel, he begged God to send down fire on his sacrifice, which he had soaked with water. Jezebel's chaplains had been totally impotent in getting Baal to send a consuming fire on theirs. Drunk with the wine of success when God did as he wished, Elijah slaughtered the three hundred priests of Baal.

However, when the Lord did not follow up and firm up the "loyalty" of the people with further attention-getters, the prophet was disgusted. He got a message from an angel that the Lord wanted to talk to him. He rehearsed his sad story of the failure to hold the loyalty of the people. And it was the Lord's fault because he wasn't doing any more of those marvelous and frightening deeds that would make them sit up and take notice. At the mountain of God where the meeting was to take place, he asked for an appointment. He was answered with an earthquake, a cyclone and a devastating fire. Cheered by the newly found dramatic talent of the Lord, giving portents of the fearful events to come, the prophet was totally deflated to hear a voice which accompanied each of the three disasters, that God was not in any of them.

Then came what the Hebrew text calls "the voice of a whispering breeze" from which the Lord spoke. Even Elijah, the prototype of the prophet, had to learn that though the Lord may occasionally manifest himself in startling and dramatic ways, at other times he may come in the voice of the whispering breeze. We had better be alert to it, or we may miss it.

CHAPTER FORTY-TWO

ADAPTATION OR COMPROMISE? (17:1–6)

Then one of the seven angels who had the seven bowls came and said to me, "Come, I will show you the judgment of the great whore who is seated on many waters, with whom the kings of the earth have committed fornication, and with the wine of whose fornication the inhabitants of the earth have become drunk." So he carried me away in the spirit into a wilderness, and I saw a woman sitting on a scarlet beast that was full of blasphemous names, and it had seven heads and ten horns. The woman was clothed in purple and scarlet, and adorned with gold and jewels and pearls, holding in her hand a golden cup full of abominations and the impurities of her fornication; and on her forehead was written a name, a mystery: "Babylon the great, mother of whores and of earth's abominations." And I saw that the woman was drunk with the blood of the saints and the blood of the witnesses to Jesus.

When Jesus sends the apostles forth to "Go, make disciples of all nations," and when they followed this "great mandate," they were confronted with a dilemma: How could the message of Jesus be adapted to new cultures and civilizations? And, more to the point, when did adaptation, so legitimate and necessary, become watering down or compromise?

The very fact that the first communities produced four Gospels, each one adapted to their own needs, shows that they took seriously the mandate to preach the gospel. It clearly indicates their awareness that Jesus and his message had to be adapted and made relevant to each unique culture and political situation. Without that adaptation, the gospel would have been irrelevant. Mark adapted his vision of Jesus and his message to his own community. Then Matthew and Luke both adapted Mark's Gospel to the language, signs, symbols and thought patterns of their particular communities. That is why we have so many differences and variations in the four Gospels.

Paul had insisted on that process of adaptation and assimilation even before Mark wrote his Gospel. It was a major exercise in adaptation for him to transpose the gospel from the Jewish to the Gentile world. His letter to the Galatians shows that the Jerusalem church saw his efforts as watering down and destroying the gospel, and he was labeled a false apostle. At great personal cost, Paul endured the suspicions and unjust accusations from his fellow Christians. We owe it to Paul that the church today is a "new creation" and not a sect of Judaism.

Right to the end of his life, about thirty years after the Ascension of Jesus, Paul brought the gospel to the citizens of the Roman Empire. He had no doubt that the mandate of Jesus, and the rights and duties of being a Roman citizen, were not only compatible, but complementary. His claim to Roman citizenship was his proud boast (Acts 22:27–28). He had not yet experienced the madness of Nero, resulting in his own death, nor the fury of Emperor Domitian, who in the ninth decade A.D. demanded to be worshiped as a god. The Roman Empire of Paul's experience, by its communication and transportation systems, had enabled him to preach the gospel to the whole world (at that time, the Roman Empire).

For the apostle to the gentiles, the Empire was a grace that made possible the great mandate of making disciples of all nations that Jesus left to the church. Hence it was deserving of loyalty and respect.

> Let every person be subject to the governing authorities; for there is no authority except from God, and those authorities that exist have been instituted by God. Therefore whoever resists authority resists what God has appointed, and those who resist will incur judgment. For rulers are not a terror to good conduct, but to bad. Do you wish to have no fear of the authority? Then do what is good, and you will receive its approval; for it is God's servant for your good. But if you do what is wrong, you should be afraid, for the authority does not bear the sword in vain! It is the servant of God to execute wrath on the wrongdoer. Therefore one must be

subject, not only because of wrath but also because of conscience. For the same reason you also pay taxes, for the authorities are God's servants, busy with this very thing. Pay to all what is due them—taxes to whom taxes are due, revenue to whom revenue is due, respect to whom respect is due, honor to whom honor is due. (Romans 13:1–7)

Thirty years later, the author of the Apocalypse, also inspired by the Holy Spirit, insists that Christians must oppose and resist the demands of the Empire with every fiber of their being. The empire, once a means of promoting the gospel, had become its enemy and was incompatible with it. The demand for emperor worship was a direct attack on the gospel that Jesus is Lord. The government is described in the foulest language. She is the whore of Babylon, and her policy is fornication.

REFLECTION

The New Testament experience bears witness to the fact that the church must be constantly alert to her prophetic role. Loyalty to the state must not blind her to policies that may be alien to the values of her Lord. It is of the very nature of the church to be constantly adapting to, and yet constantly questioning the society into which it sinks her roots. That is why Pope John XXIII convened the Second Vatican Council.

The People of God believes that it is led by the spirit of the Lord, who fills the earth. Motivated by this faith, it labors to decipher authentic signs of God's presence and purpose in the happenings, needs and desires in which this People has a part along with all other peoples of our age. For faith throws a new light on everything, manifests God's design for our total vocation, and thus directs the mind to solutions that are fully human.

This Council, first of all wishes to assess in this light those values which are most highly prized today, and to relate them to their divine source. For insofar as they stem from endowments conferred by God on humanity, these values are exceedingly good.

Yet they are often wrenched from their rightful function by the taint in man's heart, and hence stand in need of purification. (*The Church Today,* 11)

CHAPTER FORTY-THREE

ETERNAL EMPIRES? (17:6–18)

When I saw her, I was greatly amazed. But the angel said to me, "Why are you so amazed? I will tell you the mystery of the woman, and of the beast with seven heads and ten horns that carries her. The beast that you saw was, and is not, and is about to ascend from the bottomless pit and go to destruction. And the inhabitants of the earth, whose names have not been written in the book of life from the foundation of the world, will be amazed when they see the beast, because it was and is not and is to come.

This calls for a mind that has wisdom: the seven heads are seven mountains on which the woman is seated; also, they are seven kings, of whom five have fallen, one is living, and the other has not yet come; and when he comes, he must remain only a little while. As for the beast that was and is not, it is an eighth but it belongs to the seven, and it goes to destruction. And the ten horns that you saw are ten kings who have not yet received a kingdom, but they are to receive authority as kings for one hour, together with the beast. These are united in yielding their power and authority to the beast; they will make war on the Lamb, and the Lamb will conquer them, for he is Lord of lords and King of kings, and those with him are called and chosen and faithful."

And he said to me, "The waters that you saw, where the whore is seated, are peoples and multitudes and nations and languages. And the ten horns that you saw, they and the beast will hate the whore; they will make her desolate and naked; they will devour her flesh and burn her up with fire. For God has put it into their hearts to carry out his purpose by agreeing to give their kingdom to the beast, until the words of God will be fulfilled. The woman you saw is the great city that rules over the kings of the earth."

At the time of writing of the Book of Revelation, the Roman Empire was the most powerful force on earth. What had been other great empires were now mere colonies of Rome. The Romans looked upon the Mediterranean which once sent its waves on the shores of seemingly invincible empires, as *Mare Nostrum* (Our Sea). The three great empires of Greece, Syria and Egypt, once the undivided empire of Alexander the Great were now Roman colonies. Alexander had brought to an end Cyrus' Persian Empire, which had demolished the Babylonian Empire, which had brought to its knees the Assyrian Empire which had succeeded the Hittite Empire, and so on. The author of the Book of Revelation needed only a cursory knowledge of past empires to come to the conclusion that the kingdom of the Beast, the empire in which his community was suffering so much, was not invincible, incorruptible or eternal.

The fall of empires: Babylonian, Roman, Assyrian, Hittite, Syrian, Egyptian, Persian, Holy Roman, the Third Reich, Communism and even the British Empire upon which "the sun never set" are gone. They are the stuff of memories and the raw material for historians. They are no more. Of all the empires, the only one to survive is the one that he himself preached: the kingdom of God.

But what the author instinctively knew is not evident to historians: Governments, no matter how powerful they have become, are self-destructive when they start competing with the Lord. Arrogance, self-righteousness, pride, even patriotism exaggerated to nationalism, and reliance on the military-industrial complex are internal diseases and they are mortal. The author didn't need a revelation to compose these verses. He needed only an awareness of where this human race had been and what happened to the seemingly omnipotent empires it created.

REFLECTION

Have you not known? Have you not heard?
> Has it not been told you from the beginning?
> Have you not understood from the foundations of the earth?
It is he who sits above the circle of the earth,
> and its inhabitants are like grasshoppers;

who stretches out the heavens like a curtain,
    and spreads them like a tent to live in;
who brings princes to naught,
    and makes the rulers of the earth as nothing.

Scarcely are they planted, scarcely sown,
    scarcely has their stem taken root in the earth,
when he blows upon them, and they wither,
    and the tempest carries them off like stubble.

To whom then will you compare me,
    or who is my equal? says the Holy One.
Lift up your eyes on high and see:
    Who created these?
He who brings out their host and numbers them,
    calling them all by name;
because he is great in strength,
    mighty in power,
    not one is missing.

Why do you say, O Jacob,
    and speak, O Israel,
"My way is hidden from the LORD,
    and my right is disregarded by my God"?
Have you not known? Have you not heard?
The LORD is the everlasting God,
    the Creator of the ends of the earth.
He does not faint or grow weary;
    his understanding is unsearchable.
He gives power to the faint,
    and strengthens the powerless.
Even youths will faint and be weary,
    and the young will fall exhausted;
but those who wait for the LORD shall renew their strength,
    they shall mount up with wings like eagles,
they shall run and not be weary,
they shall walk and not faint. (Isaiah 40:21–31)

CHAPTER FORTY-FOUR

HUBRIS (18:1–8)

After this I saw another angel coming down from heaven, having great authority; and the earth was made bright with his splendor. He called out with a mighty voice,
"Fallen, fallen is Babylon the great!
It has become a dwelling place of demons,
a haunt of every foul spirit,
a haunt of every foul bird,
a haunt of every foul and hateful beast.
For all the nations have drunk
of the wine of the wrath of her fornication,
and the kings of the earth have committed fornication with her,
and the merchants of the earth have grown rich from the powerof her luxury."
Then I heard another voice from heaven saying,
"Come out of her, my people,
so that you do not take part in her sins,
and so that you do not share
in her plagues;
for her sins are heaped high as heaven,
and God has remembered her iniquities.
Render to her as she herself has rendered,
and repay her double for her deeds;
mix a double draught for her in the cup she mixed. As she glorified herself and lived luxuriously,
so give her a like measure of torment and grief.
Since in her heart she says,
'I rule as a queen;
I am no widow,

> and I will never see grief,'
> therefore her plagues will come in a single day—
>   pestilence and mourning and famine—
> and she will be burned with fire;
>   for mighty is the Lord God who judges her."

Arrogance is the name of the game. It is the occupational hazard of the powerful and mighty, the rich and famous, of those who glorify themselves and live luxuriously. It is the hubris of which Greek tragedies are made. It is the downfall of every nation, empire, community and individual.

Jesus saw it as the enemy of the kingdom of his Father and told a parable about an arrogant man:

> There was a rich man who was dressed in purple and fine linen and who feasted sumptuously every day. And at his gate lay a poor man named Lazarus, covered with sores, who longed to satisfy his hunger with what fell from the rich man's table; even the dogs would come and lick his sores. The poor man died and was carried away by the angels to be with Abraham. The rich man also died and was buried. (Luke 16:19–22)

And we all know the end of the story. As the author said (above) of Rome: "Mighty is the Lord God who judges her."

The opposite of arrogance is to be found in what has been called Jesus' self-portrait: the Beatitudes.

> Blessed are the poor in spirit, for theirs is the kingdom of heaven.

> Blessed are those who mourn, for they will be comforted.

> Blessed are the meek, for they will inherit the earth.

> Blessed are those who hunger and thirst for righteousness, for they will be filled.

> Blessed are the merciful, for they will receive mercy.

> Blessed are the pure in heart, for they will see God.

Blessed are the peacemakers, for they will be called children of God.

Blessed are those who are persecuted for righteousness' sake, for theirs is the kingdom of heaven.

Blessed are you when people revile you and persecute you and utter all kinds of evil against you falsely on my account. Rejoice and be glad, for your reward is great in heaven, for in the same way they persecuted the prophets who were before you. (Matthew 5:3–11)

Each beatitude is but one aspect of the face of Jesus who said: "Learn from me; for I am gentle and humble in heart, and you will find rest for your souls" (Matthew 11:29).

It is this humility that is so necessary for those who would enter God's kingdom. It can only happen when we allow God to strip away arrogance, pretence, smugness, self-righteousness, sham, self-deception and hypocrisy—even to quit demanding what we think are our rights. Humility is so hard to define, but like arrogance, you know it when you see it. Jesus' Mother is a prime example of humility and she sang about it:

He has shown strength with his arm;
>   he has scattered the proud in the thoughts of their hearts.
He has brought down the powerful from their thrones,
>   and lifted up the lowly;
> he has filled the hungry with good things,
>   and sent the rich away empty. (Luke 1:51–53)

From what he saw in his Mother, his first disciple, Jesus was able to tell us what is the attitude we must have for the kingdom: "Whoever becomes humble like this child is the greatest in the kingdom of heaven" (Matthew 18:4).

But his own experience in his ministry led him face to face with the worst kind of arrogance, that of the professional religious. This is undoubtedly what Jesus had in mind when he talked about the unforgivable sin: "Therefore I tell you, people will be forgiven for every sin and blasphemy, but blasphemy against the Spirit will not be forgiven" (Matthew 12:31). Arrogance involves such self-righteousness that it blinds one to the need of even asking for forgiveness.

Later on, Paul, who was converted from the arrogance of religious self-righteousness, would tell of the importance of humility:

> Do nothing from selfish ambition or conceit, but in humility regard others as better than yourselves. Let each of you look not to your own interests, but to the interests of others. Let the same mind be in you that was in Christ Jesus,
> who, though he was in the form of God,
> > did not regard equality with God
> > as something to be exploited,
> but emptied himself,
> taking the form of a slave,
> being born in human likeness.
> And being found in human form,
> > he humbled himself. (Philippians 2:3–8)

The author of the Book of Revelation was right on target when he identified arrogance as the enemy of humility. It made the Roman Empire of his day the antithesis of the kingdom of God.

REFLECTION

You delight me when there is room only for me in your heart!
You delight me when you are disturbed because I am not loved!
You delight me when you are at peace, knowing that I am your Abba!
You delight me when you yearn for me more than for food or drink!
You delight me when you are an instrument of my loving kindness!
You delight me when you have a one-track mind, and it is on me!
You delight me when you bring peace and fullness of life to others!
You delight me when you bear your cross, leading to fullness of life!

CHAPTER FORTY-FIVE

THE EYE OF THE NEEDLE (18:9–24)

And the kings of the earth, who committed fornication and lived in luxury with her, will weep and wail over her when they see the smoke of her burning; they will stand far off, in fear of her torment, and say,

> "Alas, alas, the great city,
> > Babylon, the mighty city!
> For in one hour your judgment has come."

And the merchants of the earth weep and mourn for her, since no one buys their cargo anymore, cargo of gold, silver, jewels and pearls, fine linen, purple, silk and scarlet, all kinds of scented wood, all articles of ivory, all articles of costly wood, bronze, iron, and marble, cinnamon, spice, incense, myrrh, frankincense, wine, olive oil, choice flour and wheat, cattle and sheep, horses and chariots, slaves—and human lives.

> "The fruit for which your soul longed
> > has gone from you,
> and all your dainties and your splendor
> > are lost to you,
> > > never to be found again!"

The merchants of these wares, who gained wealth from her, will stand far off, in fear of her torment, weeping and mourning aloud,

> "Alas, alas, the great city,
> > clothed in fine linen,
> > > in purple and scarlet,
> > adorned with gold,
> > > with jewels, and with pearls!
> For in one hour all this wealth has been laid waste!"

And all shipmasters and seafarers, sailors and all whose trade
is on the sea, stood far off and cried out as they saw the smoke of
her burning,

"What city was like the great city?"
And they threw dust on their heads, as they wept and mourned,
crying out,

"Alas, alas, the great city,
where all who had ships at sea
grew rich by her wealth!
For in one hour she has been laid waste.
Rejoice over her, O heaven,
you saints and apostles and prophets!
For God has given judgment for you against her."

Then a mighty angel took up a stone like a great millstone
and threw it into the sea, saying,

"With such violence Babylon the great city
will be thrown down,
and will be found no more;
and the sound of harpists and minstrels and of flutists and
trumpeters
will be heard in you no more;
and an artisan of any trade
will be found in you no more;
and the sound of the millstone
will be heard in you no more;
and the light of a lamp
will shine in you no more;
and the voice of bridegroom and bride
will be heard in you no more;
for your merchants were the magnates of the earth,
and all nations were deceived by your sorcery.
And in you was found the blood of prophets and of saints,
and of all who have been slaughtered on earth."

What was it that fed the arrogance of the Roman Empire (a.k.a. Babylon)? It was her incredible wealth and prosperity. The Dow Jones index on the Wall Street of Rome at the turn of the first century had gone through the ceiling. No nation before her had seen such an accumulation of wealth. On the mainland, near Patmos where Revelation was written, were the Roman colonies that were the seven churches of the Apocalypse. The words that the author addresses to Laodicea could have been a universal warning, even to the ends of the empire. "For you say, 'I am rich, I have prospered, and I need nothing.' You do not realize that you are wretched, pitiable, poor, blind, and naked" (Revelation 3:17).

Wealth and prosperity contain the seeds of infidelity. The Book of Deuteronomy had warned God's own people hundreds of years before: "For when I have brought them into the land flowing with milk and honey, which I promised on oath to their ancestors, and they have eaten their fill and grown fat, they will turn to other gods and serve them, despising me and breaking my covenant" (31:20).

Wealth and prosperity are more often a sign of sickness than health. It is not that riches are evil, but that they engender the supercilious attitude that they are a sign of God's approval. Riches are looked upon as a reward from God who has a special fondness for us. And he does have good taste for he has prospered us. We are living proof that God knows what he is doing (and therefore we can do anything, because he is on our side!).

The "lifestyle of the rich and famous" that accompanies prosperity can be so dangerous that Ezekiel told an alternate account of the fall of the human race based upon it.

> The word of the LORD came to me saying: Mortal, say to the
> prince of Tyre...
>> "Because your heart is proud
>>> and you have said, 'I am a god;
>> I sit in the seat of the gods,
>>> in the heart of the seas,'
>> yet you are but a mortal, and no god,
>>> though you compare your mind
>>> with the mind of a god

...
>
> you have amassed wealth for yourself,
> and have gathered gold and silver
> into your treasuries.
> By your great wisdom in trade
> you have increased your wealth,
> and your heart has become proud in your wealth
>
> ...
>
> Will you still say, "I am a god,"
> in the presence of those who kill you,
> though you are but a mortal, and no god,
> in the hands of those who wound you?
>
> ...
>
> You were the signet of perfection,
> full of wisdom
> and perfect in beauty.
> You were in Eden, the garden of God;
> every precious stone was your covering,
>
> ...
>
> You were blameless in your ways
> from the day that you were created,
> until iniquity was found in you.
> In the abundance of your trade
> you were filled with violence, and you sinned;
> so I cast you as a profane thing from the mountain of God,
> and the guardian cherub drove you out
> from among the stones of fire." (28:1–5, 9, 12–13, 15–16)

The author of Revelation had only to consult with his fellow prophet Ezekiel to find out what the Roman Empire's problem was. We know it as "original sin." And the only remedy? "...to all who received him, who believed in his name, he gave power to become children of God" (John 1:12).

REFLECTION

Wealth is not intrinsically evil, but it is extremely dangerous. When Jesus blesses the "poor in spirit" he is not beatifying them for keeping a minimum balance in their bank account. The question is not how much do you possess, but what possesses you? What makes you tick? What is your priority? He was so adamant about this that he startled his listeners by saying that it was easier for a camel to pass through the eye of a needle than for a rich man to get into heaven. He wasn't trying to get a laugh, except from those who missed the point. He was deadly serious.

Pope John Paul II echoed his Lord when he said: "This is one of the constant temptations of humanity: attaching oneself to money, regarding it as endowed with an invincible force; it deludes one into thinking that death can also be bought, removing it from oneself" (Audience of 10/27/04).

As a perceptive wit asked, "Did you ever see a U-Haul trailer being pulled by a hearse?"

CHAPTER FORTY-SIX

JESUS' WEDDING! (19:1–10)

After this I heard what seemed to be the loud voice of a great multitude in heaven, saying,

"Hallelujah!

Salvation and glory and power to our God,

for his judgments are true and just;

he has judged the great whore

who corrupted the earth with her fornication,

and he has avenged on her the blood of his servants."

Once more they said,

"Hallelujah!

The smoke goes up from her forever and ever."

And the twenty-four elders and the four living creatures fell down and worshiped God who is seated on the throne, saying,

"Amen. Hallelujah!"

And from the throne came a voice saying,

"Praise our God,

all you his servants,

and all who fear him,

small and great."

Then I heard what seemed to be the voice of a great multitude, like the sound of many waters and like the sound of mighty thunder peals, crying out,

"Hallelujah!

For the Lord our God

the Almighty reigns.

Let us rejoice and exult

and give him the glory,

for the marriage of the Lamb has come,

and his bride has made herself ready;

> to her it has been granted to be clothed
> with fine linen, bright and pure"—

for the fine linen is the righteous deeds of the saints.

And the angel said to me, "Write this: Blessed are those who are invited to the marriage supper of the Lamb." And he said to me, "These are true words of God." Then I fell down at his feet to worship him, but he said to me, "You must not do that! I am a fellow servant with you and your comrades who hold the testimony of Jesus. Worship God! For the testimony of Jesus is the spirit of prophecy."

When the glory of its Alleluias (the source for Handel's "Alleluia Chorus") fades away, this passage makes two important points: (1) even for the most spiritual person, idolatry (letting something or someone other than Jesus take control) is a constant temptation, and (2) the bond of a beautiful marriage is one of the greatest signs to let us know what our union with Jesus is like.

The author makes the mistake of worshiping the messenger rather than him who sent it. It shows how easily religious people can fall into idolatry, even of religious things. The Pharisees' opposition to Jesus and the church of the gospels, resulted from their making an idol out of the precepts of the law. Jesus' critique of them results from their misplaced loyalty and faith. Preserving the status quo of the structures of religion became more important than love and the God who is love.

> Woe to you, scribes and Pharisees, hypocrites! For you tithe mint, dill, and cummin, and have neglected the weightier matters of the law (Torah, or God's will): justice and mercy and faith. It is these you ought to have practiced without neglecting the others. You blind guides! You strain out a gnat but swallow a camel!
>
> Woe to you, scribes and Pharisees, hypocrites! For you clean the outside of the cup and of the plate, but inside they are full of greed and self-indulgence. You blind Pharisee! First clean the inside of the cup, so that the outside also may become clean. (Matthew 23:23–26)

Even zeal for the minutiae of religious observance can become idolatry, eclipsing the spiritual embrace of the God who loves.

A popular novel recently featured the marriage of Jesus to Mary Magdalene. It cannot be emphasized too strongly that this was a figment of the author's imagination, utterly without historical fact or foundation. The media had a field day accusing the church of concealing the "revelation" which appealed to those who love the sensational, even if it contains not the slightest grain of truth.

This passage of the Book of Revelation, however, does refer to the marriage feast of Jesus. But the bride is his church. This analogy has a deep and powerful meaning especially for those who have experienced or at least observed closely a wonderful marriage, full of love and fidelity. It is no surprise that Jesus in both his parables and preaching often used human love and marriage to let us know of life with him in the kingdom. For John it is such an important point that he begins the ministry of Jesus (his invitation to love) with the wedding feast of Cana. Weddings and bridesmaids and nuptial banquets are an important part of his vocabulary. "The kingdom of God is like…" means that "God's love for us is like…" (fill in the blanks!). And so the author continues the great prophetic tradition, using marriage, both successful and disastrous, as the best sign of our union with God (Hosea 1 and Ezekiel 24).

Paul continues the tradition:

> …husbands should love their wives as they do their own bodies. He who loves his wife loves himself. For no one ever hates his own body, but he nourishes and tenderly cares for it, just as Christ does for the church, because we are members of his body. "For this reason a man will leave his father and mother and be joined to his wife, and the two will become one flesh." This is a great mystery, and I am applying it to Christ and the church. (Ephesians 5:28–32)

REFLECTION

Christ the Lord abundantly blessed this many-faceted love, welling up as it does from the fountain of divine love, and structured as it is on the model of His union with His Church. For as God of old made Himself present to his people through a covenant of love and fidelity so now the Savior of men and the Spouse of the Church comes into lives of married Christians through the sacrament of matrimony. He abides with them thereafter so that just as He loved the Church and handed Himself over on her behalf, the spouses may love each other with perpetual fidelity through mutual self-bestowal....

Finally, let the spouses themselves, made to the image of the living God, and enjoying the authentic dignity of persons, be joined to one another in equal affection, harmony of mind and the work of mutual sanctification. Thus, following Christ who is the principle of life, by the sacrifices and joys of their vocation and through their faithful love, married people can become witnesses of the mystery of love which the Lord revealed to the world by His dying and His rising up to life. (*Constitution on the Church in the Modern World*, 48, 52)

CHAPTER FORTY-SEVEN

THE TRIUMPH OF 777 (19:11–21)

Then I saw heaven opened, and there was a white horse! Its rider is called Faithful and True, and in righteousness he judges and makes war. His eyes are like a flame of fire, and on his head are many diadems; and he has a name inscribed that no one knows but himself. He is clothed in a robe dipped in blood, and his name is called The Word of God. And the armies of heaven, wearing fine linen, white and pure, were following him on white horses. From his mouth comes a sharp sword with which to strike down the nations, and he will rule them with a rod of iron; he will tread the wine press of the fury of the wrath of God the Almighty. On his robe and on his thigh he has a name inscribed, "King of kings and Lord of lords."

Then I saw an angel standing in the sun, and with a loud voice he called to all the birds that fly in midheaven, "Come, gather for the great supper of God, to eat the flesh of kings, the flesh of captains, the flesh of the mighty, the flesh of horses and their riders—flesh of all, both free and slave, both small and great." Then I saw the beast and the kings of the earth with their armies gathered to make war against the rider on the horse and against his army. And the beast was captured, and with it the false prophet who had performed in its presence the signs by which he deceived those who had received the mark of the beast and those who worshiped its image. These two were thrown alive into the lake of fire that burns with sulfur. And the rest were killed by the sword of the rider on the horse, the sword that came from his mouth; and all the birds were gorged with their flesh.

Even though a great mind like Saint Augustine's was seduced by the flesh before his conversion, there is no foundation whatsoever in all of God's revelation for a dualistic Manichaeism. Sometimes it may seem that we poor mortals are caught in the crossfire between a god of good and a god of evil. But it just isn't so. Our God is in charge, despite appearances to the contrary. The bottom line is that his Son, the Word, is "King of kings and Lord of lords." No exceptions. No one has to ask: "Who's in charge here?" There is no doubt and no contest. Jesus is Lord!

It was not for nothing that the church placed his birthday on December 25, to replace the feast of the unconquered sun. He is the unconquered Son! What the prologue of Saint John promised is now fulfilled:

> He was in the beginning with God. All things came into being through him, and without him not one thing came into being. What has come into being in him was life, and the life was the light of all people. The light shines in the darkness, and the darkness did not overcome it. (John 1:2–5)

God has no competition. We may not have been able to see it clearly, but he has been in charge from the get-go. And because of our union with Christ, his victory is our own. "Whatever is born of God conquers the world. And this is the victory that conquers the world, our faith. Who is it that conquers the world but the one who believes that Jesus is the Son of God?" (1 John 5:4)

While the author's imagery of the carrion birds consuming the flesh of those who empowered the "evil empire" may be alien to our way of thinking (and even of Jesus' plea for forgiveness to enemies), the point is well taken that he who conquered death is in the process of overcoming all that smacks of death.

> …all will be made alive in Christ. But each in his own order: Christ the first fruits, then at his coming those who belong to Christ. Then comes the end, when he hands over the kingdom to God the Father, after he has destroyed every ruler and every authority and power. For he must reign until he has put all his enemies under his feet. The last enemy to be destroyed is death.

For "God has put all things in subjection under his feet." (1 Corinthians 15:22–27)

REFLECTION

If God is for us, who is against us? He who did not withhold his own Son, but gave him up for all of us, will he not with him also give us everything else? Who will bring any charge against God's elect? It is God who justifies. Who is to condemn? It is Christ Jesus, who died, yes, who was raised, who is at the right hand of God, who indeed intercedes for us. Who will separate us from the love of Christ? Will hardship, or distress, or persecution, or famine, or nakedness, or peril, or sword? As it is written,

"For your sake we are being killed all day long;
we are accounted as sheep to be slaughtered."

No, in all these things we are more than conquerors through him who loved us. For I am convinced that neither death, nor life, nor angels, nor rulers, nor things present, nor things to come, nor powers, nor height, nor depth, nor anything else in all creation, will be able to separate us from the love of God in Christ Jesus our Lord. (Romans 8:31–39)

CHAPTER FORTY-EIGHT

THE THOUSAND YEARS (20:1–10)

Then I saw an angel coming down from heaven, holding in his hand the key to the bottomless pit and a great chain. He seized the dragon, that ancient serpent, who is the Devil and Satan, and bound him for a thousand years, and threw him into the pit, and locked and sealed it over him, so that he would deceive the nations no more, until the thousand years were ended. After that he must be let out for a little while.

Then I saw thrones, and those seated on them were given authority to judge. I also saw the souls of those who had been beheaded for their testimony to Jesus and for the word of God. They had not worshiped the beast or its image and had not received its mark on their foreheads or their hands. They came to life and reigned with Christ a thousand years. (The rest of the dead did not come to life until the thousand years were ended.) This is the first resurrection. Blessed and holy are those who share in the first resurrection. Over these the second death has no power, but they will be priests of God and of Christ, and they will reign with him a thousand years.

When the thousand years are ended, Satan will be released from his prison and will come out to deceive the nations at the four corners of the earth, Gog and Magog, in order to gather them for battle; they are as numerous as the sands of the sea. They marched up over the breadth of the earth and surrounded the camp of the saints and the beloved city. And fire came down from heaven and consumed them. And the devil who had deceived them was thrown into the lake of fire and sulfur, where the beast and the false prophet were, and they will be tormented day and night forever and ever.

Crux interpretum is a Latin expression to signify a very difficult passage for interpreters. This passage about the thousand-year reign of Christ is not difficult. It is impossible. Millions of fundamentalist Christians have been excommunicated from their churches over its interpretation.

To take it at face value (and we don't do that with any of the other highly symbolic passages in the book) is to think that our God behaves like the pagan gods of Rome do. They played games with earthlings. They enjoyed watching their human toys twist and turn trying to figure out the unpredictable and capricious next move from heaven. And since the emperor had proclaimed his own divine nature, he was one of the operators and not one of the victims of the game. It almost seems as if this were written by the emperor, giving himself a reprieve. It smells of satanic "business as usual."

The time frame is a big question. Is the period of the "thousand years" in the past, going on, or in the future? And does it mean just a thousand years? Is the reign of Christ, followed by the release of evil forces something that is over? Jesus did say "I watched Satan fall from heaven like a flash of lightning" (Luke 10:18). So, after Christ has conquered the force of evil, why would they be set free again? Perhaps it is to remind even the saints, while we are upon this earth, there is no "Star Wars shield" that is an absolute defense against all evil because it is cunning, baffling and powerful. We must always be aware of the constant danger of letting down our guard. Mediocrity and smugness are the doorkeepers who let in the forces of evil.

Paul's advice to the Philippians has lost none of its urgency:

> Therefore, my beloved, just as you have always obeyed me, not only in my presence, but much more now in my absence, work out your own salvation with fear and trembling; for it is God who is at work in you, enabling you both to will and to work for his good pleasure. (Philippians 2:12–13)

And Yahweh's warning to Cain about the insidiousness of sin that is always "lurking at the door" (Genesis 4:7) is old, but far from old-fashioned!

Nor have the words to the church in Laodicea lost their force. They still speak to us:

> And to the angel of the church in Laodicea write: The words of the Amen, the faithful and true witness, the origin of God's creation:
>
> "I know your works; you are neither cold nor hot. I wish that you were either cold or hot. So, because you are lukewarm, and neither cold nor hot, I am about to spit you out of my mouth. For you say, 'I am rich, I have prospered, and I need nothing.' You do not realize that you are wretched, pitiable, poor, blind, and naked." (Revelation 3:14–17)

REFLECTION

This passage is a good reminder that God's word was primarily addressed to his people almost two thousand years ago. Their thought patterns, frames of reference and literary forms are quite different from our own. Sometimes, even after much work, we cannot find out what they understood by a text when they first heard it (Gog and Magog?), or what the author intended to say. There is such a cache of meaning and treasure of truth in the rest of God's word that it is frustrating when we cannot penetrate a portion of it. Perhaps a given passage (like Paul's mention of being baptized for the dead [1 Corinthians 15:29]) was intended by God to have a meaning only for the time in which it was first written. Or perhaps it is one more thing to add to our list of questions that we will have for God when we enter the New Jerusalem. For now, we are in good company, because even the early Christians seem to have had some confusion about the last days.

Still, in that confusion, there is the truth given:

> Therefore, beloved, while you are waiting for these things, strive to be found by him at peace, without spot or blemish; and regard the patience of our Lord as salvation. So also our beloved brother Paul wrote to you according to the wisdom given him, speaking of this as he does in all his letters. There are some things in them

hard to understand, which the ignorant and unstable twist to their own destruction, as they do the other scriptures. You therefore, beloved, since you are forewarned, beware that you are not carried away with the error of the lawless and lose your own stability. But grow in the grace and knowledge of our Lord and Savior Jesus Christ. To him be the glory both now and to the day of eternity. Amen. (2 Peter 3:14–18)

CHAPTER FORTY-NINE

THE BEGINNING OF THE END (20:11–15)

> Then I saw a great white throne and the one who sat on it; the
> earth and the heaven fled from his presence, and no place was
> found for them. And I saw the dead, great and small, standing
> before the throne, and books were opened. Also another book was
> opened, the book of life. And the dead were judged according to
> their works, as recorded in the books. And the sea gave up the
> dead that were in it, Death and Hades gave up the dead that were
> in them, and all were judged according to what they had done.
> Then Death and Hades were thrown into the lake of fire. This is
> the second death, the lake of fire; and anyone whose name was not
> found written in the book of life was thrown into the lake of fire.

Our era has had more than its share of religious fanatics who have led their
followers apart to await the imminent coming of Christ and his judgment.
Some have ended up in disappointment and frustration, others in mass
murder and suicide. Their conduct, as bizarre as their misinterpretation of
God's will, is in no way supported or encouraged by the Word of God.
Their deluded and false interpretations, which they claim have been
revealed, result in tragic consequences that are not God's doing. Religious
fanaticism is certainly not the work of God.

To avoid that, we must remember that the best commentary on the
Bible is the Bible. We look at the passage in the context of the whole
Biblical text.

This is the light that the Gospel of John sheds on the Last Judgment:

> And whoever sees me sees him who sent me. I have come as light
> into the world, so that everyone who believes in me should not
> remain in the darkness. I do not judge anyone who hears my
> words and does not keep them, for I came not to judge the world,

but to save the world. The one who rejects me and does not receive my word has a judge; on the last day the word that I have spoken will serve as judge, for I have not spoken on my own, but the Father who sent me has himself given me a commandment about what to say and what to speak. And I know that his commandment is eternal life. What I speak, therefore, I speak just as the Father has told me. (John 12:45–50)

Very truly, I tell you, anyone who hears my word and believes him who sent me has eternal life, and does not come under judgment, but has passed from death to life. For just as the Father has life in himself, so he has granted the Son also to have life in himself; and he has given him authority to execute judgment, because he is the Son of Man. (John 5:24–26)

REFLECTION

Jesus spoke to them, saying, "I am the light of the world. Whoever follows me will never walk in darkness but will have the light of life." Then the Pharisees said to him, "You are testifying on your own behalf; your testimony is not valid." Jesus answered, "Even if I testify on my own behalf, my testimony is valid because I know where I have come from and where I am going, but you do not know where I come from or where I am going. You judge by human standards; I judge no one. Yet even if I do judge, my judgment is valid; for it is not I alone who judge, but I and the Father who sent me." (John 8:12–16)

I have come as light into the world, so that everyone who believes in me should not remain in the darkness. I do not judge anyone who hears my words and does not keep them, for I came not to judge the world, but to save the world. The one who rejects me and does not receive my word has a judge; on the last day the word that I have spoken will serve as judge. (John 12:46–48)

CHAPTER FIFTY

HEAVEN AND HELL (21:1–8)

Then I saw a new heaven and a new earth; for the first heaven and the first earth had passed away, and the sea was no more. And I saw the holy city, the new Jerusalem, coming down out of heaven from God, prepared as a bride adorned for her husband. And I heard a loud voice from the throne saying,

> "See, the home of God is among mortals.
> He will dwell with them as their God;
> they will be his peoples,
> and God himself will be with them;
> he will wipe every tear from their eyes.
> Death will be no more;
> mourning and crying and pain will be no more,
> for the first things have passed away."

And the one who was seated on the throne said, "See, I am making all things new." Also he said, "Write this, for these words are trustworthy and true." Then he said to me, "It is done! I am the Alpha and the Omega, the beginning and the end. To the thirsty I will give water as a gift from the spring of the water of life. Those who conquer will inherit these things, and I will be their God and they will be my children. But as for the cowardly, the faithless, the polluted, the murderers, the fornicators, the sorcerers, the idolaters, and all liars, their place will be in the lake that burns with fire and sulfur, which is the second death."

The cosmos in which the first Christians dwelt is imagined by the author to be so tainted and polluted that a new one will replace it. The holy city, destroyed by the Romans a quarter of a century before is also tainted, as the author has already told us: "...and their dead bodies will lie in the street of the great city that is prophetically called Sodom and Egypt, where also their Lord was crucified" (Revelation 11:8). As Jesus, "God with us" rose to newness of life, so must the city which was the sign of God's presence in the previous covenant,

> Blessed be the LORD from Zion,
> he who resides in Jerusalem. (Psalm 135:21)

The city that died in the year 70 at the hands of the Romans is thought to share in Jesus' resurrection and to be transformed symbolically for the new eternal covenant.

Since death is now only a passage to life, the grieving that accompanied it is turned into joy for those who have been faithful.

> Since, therefore, the children share flesh and blood, he himself likewise shared the same things, so that through death he might destroy the one who has the power of death, that is, the devil, and free those who all their lives were held in slavery by the fear of death. (Hebrews 2:14–15)

The author gives us a definition of hell: It is the second death. (The existentialist philosopher, Jean-Paul Sartre, maintained "hell is other people.") The stink, the fumes and the smoke are the stage props that will make life miserable for those who are perpetually dying. It is so horrible it can only be called "second death." The author borrows the imagery from the smoldering trash and garbage heap on the south side of the holy city in the valley called *Gai (ben) Hinnon* or *Gehenna*. Jesus used it for "show and tell" in Mark 9:45. Matthew 18:8 adapts the saying of Jesus and calls it "eternal fire."

It should not be forgotten, that heaven and hell are insights that were added, or at least clarified, by Jesus and his followers. In the Old Testament, the only way to achieve immortality was by living on in your children. Hence, celibacy was unthinkable, and dying childless was a disaster that the family was obliged to remedy (the levirate law or the law of the redeemer was the theme of the Book of Ruth). It is only in the New

Testament that a fully elaborated concept of states of reward and punishment in the afterlife is found. The closest the Old Testament came to it was that after death, you might find yourself in Sheol, but that was like a deep freeze.

> For in death there is no remembrance of you;
>> in Sheol who can give you praise (Psalm 6:5)

King Hezekiah, praying for a restoration to health reminds Yahweh that no praise comes from the nether world.

> For Sheol cannot thank you,
>> death cannot praise you;
> those who go down to the Pit cannot hope
>> for your faithfulness.
> The living, the living, they thank you,
>> as I do this day;
> fathers make known to children
>> your faithfulness. (Isaiah 38:18–19)

But Jesus says:

> Do not let your hearts be troubled. Believe in God, believe also in me. In my Father's house there are many dwelling places. If it were not so, would I have told you that I go to prepare a place for you? And if I go and prepare a place for you, I will come again and will take you to myself, so that where I am, there you may be also. (John 14:13)

REFLECTION

The phrase "second death," used by the author of Revelation, is not found in our modern Christian vocabulary as a synonym for hell. It was employed, however, up to medieval times when Saint Francis of Assisi used it in the concluding lines of his "Canticle of the Creatures." As he lay dying on October 3, 1226, he wrote:

Praised be you my Lord, for Our Sister, Bodily Death,
From whom no one living can escape.
Woe to those who die in mortal sin.
Blessed are those whom death will find in your most holy will,
For the second death will do them no harm.
Praise and bless my Lord and give him thanks
And serve him with great humility.

CHAPTER FIFTY-ONE

AN EDIFICE COMPLEX (21:9–27)

Then one of the seven angels who had the seven bowls full of the seven last plagues came and said to me, "Come, I will show you the bride, the wife of the Lamb." And in the spirit he carried me away to a great, high mountain and showed me the holy city Jerusalem coming down out of heaven from God. It has the glory of God and a radiance like a very rare jewel, like jasper, clear as crystal. It has a great, high wall with twelve gates, and at the gates twelve angels, and on the gates are inscribed the names of the twelve tribes of the Israelites; on the east three gates, on the north three gates, on the south three gates, and on the west three gates. And the wall of the city has twelve foundations, and on them are the twelve names of the twelve apostles of the Lamb.

The angel who talked to me had a measuring rod of gold to measure the city and its gates and walls. The city lies foursquare, its length the same as its width; and he measured the city with his rod, fifteen hundred miles; its length and width and height are equal. He also measured its wall, one hundred forty-four cubits by human measurement, which the angel was using. The wall is built of jasper, while the city is pure gold, clear as glass. The foundations of the wall of the city are adorned with every jewel; the first was jasper, the second sapphire, the third agate, the fourth emerald, the fifth onyx, the sixth carnelian, the seventh chrysolite, the eighth beryl, the ninth topaz, the tenth chrysoprase, the eleventh jacinth, the twelfth amethyst. And the twelve gates are twelve pearls, each of the gates is a single pearl, and the street of the city is pure gold, transparent as glass.

I saw no temple in the city, for its temple is the Lord God the Almighty and the Lamb. And the city has no need of sun or moon to shine on it, for the glory of God is its light, and its lamp is the

Lamb. The nations will walk by its light, and the kings of the earth will bring their glory into it. Its gates will never be shut by day—and there will be no night there. People will bring into it the glory and the honor of the nations. But nothing unclean will enter it, nor anyone who practices abomination or falsehood, but only those who are written in the Lamb's book of life.

With great poetic hyperbole, the author describes the heavenly Jerusalem. We all have our own idea of what heaven will be like but this sounds like the wishful thinking of someone musing while looking into a jeweler's window!

It is indeed a Holy City but without a temple. The earthly temple is no more, so the author turns to its celestial prototype. "For Christ did not enter a sanctuary made by human hands, a mere copy of the true one, but he entered into heaven itself, now to appear in the presence of God on our behalf" (Hebrews 9:24). But even if the earthly temple had not been destroyed by the Emperor Hadrian's son Titus in A.D. 70, it has been eclipsed. It has been replaced by another, a living temple.

For the Jewish people, the sight of the temple was proof that they were still God's people. It was a sign of his presence among them. Every Jewish male was required to visit it three times a year on the pilgrim feasts. Jesus was fulfilling that obligation when he was twelve years old, along with hundreds of thousands of his fellow Jews from Galilee.

But five hundred years before, through the prophet Jeremiah, Yahweh had warned them about putting their trust in a building.

Thus says the LORD of hosts, the God of Israel: Amend your ways and your doings, and let me dwell with you in this place. Do not trust in these deceptive words: "This is the temple of the LORD, the temple of the LORD, the temple of the LORD."...Has this house, which is called by my name, become a den of robbers in your sight? You know, I too am watching, says the LORD. (Jeremiah 7:3, 4, 11)

It was a major leap for the Jewish people to grasp that Yahweh was no longer present in a building but in a person. Even while Jesus was standing in front of it, he proclaimed: "I tell you, something greater than the temple is here" (Matthew 9:6). That he himself was the sign of the presence of God, and no longer a physical building, took a long time for his disciples to grasp.

> Jesus answered them, "Destroy this temple, and in three days I will raise it up." The Jews then said, "This temple has been under construction for forty-six years, and will you raise it up in three days?" But he was speaking of the temple of his body. After he was raised from the dead, his disciples remembered that he had said this; and they believed the scripture and the word that Jesus had spoken. (John 2:19–22)

In Mark's Gospel, at his trial, the accusation of blasphemy was made, because they could not grasp the deepest meaning of his claim:

> For many gave false testimony against him, and their testimony did not agree. Some stood up and gave false testimony against him, saying, "We heard him say, 'I will destroy this temple that is made with hands, and in three days I will build another, not made with hands.'" But even on this point their testimony did not agree. (Mark 14:56–59)

The first martyr, Saint Stephen, paid with his life for asserting that having Jesus, the temple was now superfluous:

> It was Solomon who built a house for him. Yet the Most High does not dwell in houses made with human hands; as the prophet says,
>> 'Heaven is my throne,
>>> and the earth is my footstool.
>> What kind of house will you build for me, says the Lord,
>>> or what is the place of my rest
>> Did not my hand make all these things?'

> You stiff-necked people, uncircumcised in heart and ears, you
> are forever opposing the Holy Spirit, just as your ancestors used
> to do. (Acts 7:47–51)

REFLECTION

The temple was not God. It was a sign of his presence among his people. We no longer use the word temple; we use church. The word is Saint Paul's gift to our profession of faith. Yet, in all of his epistles, he never used it in connection with a building. If he walked into our town and asked where the church was, and we showed him a building, he would collapse laughing. It is good to remember in this time of closing of buildings, that no matter how old or beautiful, they are only shelters for the church. They are not the church. The church began without buildings and will survive without them. God said: I will be your God and you will be my people. He did not say: I will be your God and you'll know it by the brick and mortar! Real faith does not permit of an "edifice complex." Even buildings can become idols!

CHAPTER FIFTY-TWO

THE RIVER OF LIFE (22:1–7)

Then the angel showed me the river of the water of life, bright as crystal, flowing from the throne of God and of the Lamb through the middle of the street of the city. On either side of the river is the tree of life with its twelve kinds of fruit, producing its fruit each month; and the leaves of the tree are for the healing of the nations. Nothing accursed will be found there any more. But the throne of God and of the Lamb will be in it, and his servants will worship him; they will see his face, and his name will be on their foreheads. And there will be no more night; they need no light of lamp or sun, for the Lord God will be their light, and they will reign forever and ever.

And he said to me, "These words are trustworthy and true, for the Lord, the God of the spirits of the prophets, has sent his angel to show his servants what must soon take place."

"See, I am coming soon! Blessed is the one who keeps the words of the prophecy of this book."

Everyone has an idea of heaven, but it is nice to know that there will be no more water bills or electric bills! The river of the water of life and the light from the glory of the Lord God are gratis. (That's being a bit literal.) But life with God is not about clear water, the fruit-of-the-month club, medicinal herbs or a source of light. However, they are all signs that God is with us. And that is what heaven is about.

Then he said to me, "It is done! I am the Alpha and the Omega, the beginning and the end. To the thirsty I will give water as a gift from the spring of the water of life" (Revelation 21:6). For those who dwell in a land where water is scarce, heaven would not be heaven without an unfailing supply of it. However, this special water is life-giving, because its source is not a mountain spring but God and his Son.

The Feast of Tabernacles, the harvest festival, celebrated light and water as the gifts of God that had made the harvest possible. Jesus was present at it and gave it a new meaning:

> Jesus spoke to them, saying, "I am the light of the world. Whoever follows me will never walk in darkness but will have the light of life."
>
> ...
>
> "On the last day of the festival, the great day, while Jesus was standing there, he cried out, "Let anyone who is thirsty come to me, and let the one who believes in me drink. As the scripture has said, 'Out of the believer's heart shall flow rivers of living water.'" Now he said this about the Spirit, which believers in him were to receive; for as yet there was no Spirit, because Jesus was not yet glorified. (John 8:12, 7:37–39ff)

As they read this, the Christians of the first century hiding under cover of darkness for the "breaking of the bread" would be reminded of how they were born again in the waters of life, life in the Holy Spirit! They would contrast this water with the water of chaos and death: the sea. We have already been told "and the sea was no more" (Revelation 21:1). There cannot be a sea of saltwater in heaven, for that is the abode of the sea monster and of chaos (Revelation 13:1). It would have been interesting if a Greek had written this passage. Unlike the people of the Old Testament, the Greeks were a seafaring people. They made their life from it. They did not see it as the source of death and destruction but of life and prosperity. The meaning and truth of a symbol can change from culture to culture and from civilization to civilization.

REFLECTION

The Holy City

Last night I lay asleeping, there came a dream so fair,
I stood in old Jerusalem, beside the temple there,
I heard the children singing, and ever as they sang,
I thought the voice of angels from heav'n in answer rang,

Jerusalem, Jerusalem, lift up your gates and sing.
Hosanna in the Highest, Hosanna to your King.
Jerusalem, Jerusalem, lift up your gates and sing.
Hosanna in the Highest, Hosanna to your King.
And then I thought my dream was changed, The streets no longer
    rang;
Hushed were the glad Hosannas the little children sang.
The sun grew dark with mystery, the earth was cold and chill,
As the shadow of a cross arose upon a lonely hill.
Jerusalem, Jerusalem, Hark how the angels sing,
Hosanna in the highest, Hosanna to your King.
Jerusalem, Jerusalem, lift up your gates and sing.
Hosanna in the Highest, Hosanna to your King.
And once again the scene was changed, New earth there seemed to be.
I saw the Holy City beside the tideless sea.
The light of God was on its streets. The gates were open wide
and all who would might enter and no one was denied.
No need of moon or stars by night or sun to shine by day.
It was the new Jerusalem that would not pass away!
Jerusalem, Jerusalem, sing for the night is o'er,
Hosanna in the highest, Hosanna forevermore,
Hosanna in the highest, Hosanna forevermore.
(Stephen Adam, 1892)

CHAPTER FIFTY-THREE

TEMPTED BY IDOLS (22:8–16)

I, John, am the one who heard and saw these things. And when I heard and saw them, I fell down to worship at the feet of the angel who showed them to me; but he said to me, "You must not do that! I am a fellow servant with you and your comrades the prophets, and with those who keep the words of this book. Worship God!"

And he said to me, "Do not seal up the words of the prophecy of this book, for the time is near. Let the evildoer still do evil, and the filthy still be filthy, and the righteous still do right, and the holy still be holy."

"See, I am coming soon; my reward is with me, to repay according to everyone's work. I am the Alpha and the Omega, the first and the last, the beginning and the end."

Blessed are those who wash their robes, so that they will have the right to the tree of life and may enter the city by the gates. Outside are the dogs and sorcerers and fornicators and murderers and idolaters, and everyone who loves and practices falsehood. "It is I, Jesus, who sent my angel to you with this testimony for the churches. I am the root and the descendant of David, the bright morning star."

The whole thrust of the Book of Revelation is to condemn the Empire for forcing the idolatry of emperor worship on the Christians. How ironic it is, then, that the author confesses to his readers that he himself almost fell into idolatry of a different kind. It is a startling warning that professional religious have the occupational hazard of making the things of religion objects of a cult.

Here it is worship of the messenger rather than of the Lord who sent him. For those who so opposed Jesus, it was the worship of the law rather than him whose will it embodied. The conversion of Saint Paul is all about turning away from this idolatry. "…as to the law, a Pharisee; as to zeal, a persecutor of the church; as to righteousness under the law, blameless" (Philippians 3:5). The Jerusalem temple had also become the object of idolatry (as with some of today's church buildings). Jeremiah had long ago warned against putting one's trust in it instead of in the Lord. "Do not trust in these deceptive words: 'This is the temple of the LORD, the temple of the LORD, the temple of the LORD'" (Jeremiah 7:4). Jeremiah suffered for naming the idol, and Jesus was condemned to death for "blasphemy": "Some stood up and gave false testimony against him, saying, 'We heard him say, "I will destroy this temple that is made with hands, and in three days I will build another, not made with hands"'" (Mark 14:57–58).

It has been said that the seven last words of the church are: "We never did it that way before." While the Catholic church has rightly held on to the role of tradition in God's revelation, customs have crept in and been assimilated into it which never came from God; nor were they part of Tradition (capital T) thus being designated holy and unchangeable. As Saint Thomas More said in *A Man for All Seasons:* there was nothing holy or sacred about the ancient Latin language. Even Jesus did not speak it. It was not part of Tradition. It was just old.

It may also be that the author has become susceptible to idolatry of another kind. For example, verse 11 says: "Let the evildoer still do evil, and the filthy still be filthy, and the righteous still do right, and the holy still be holy." This shows that he has not let go of the primitive and simplistic Old Testament thinking that seems more appropriate to a child than to a prophet. God's omnipotence is emphasized at the expense of his people's free will. It sounds like there is no possibility of conversion. It is so hard to change ways of thinking, and so easy to make idols of them! "We never did it that way before!"

However, the beatitude of verse 14: "Blessed are those who wash their robes, so that they will have the right to the tree of life and may enter the city by the gates," shows that he is on the right path. The blessed are free to don their cleansed baptismal robes and choose to enter into life and the presence of God.

REFLECTION

The conversion of Saint Paul was about change, about letting go. His declaration of independence from the old so that he could embrace the new is found in his Letter to the Galatians. But he recognizes that such adaptation has its pitfalls. It can be done for selfish or misguided motives.

> For freedom Christ has set us free. Stand firm, therefore, and do not submit again to a yoke of slavery....
>
> For you were called to freedom, brothers and sisters; only do not use your freedom as an opportunity for self-indulgence, but through love become slaves to one another. For the whole law is summed up in a single commandment, "You shall love your neighbor as yourself." If, however, you bite and devour one another, take care that you are not consumed by one another.
>
> Live by the Spirit, I say, and do not gratify the desires of the flesh. For what the flesh desires is opposed to the Spirit, and what the Spirit desires is opposed to the flesh; for these are opposed to each other, to prevent you from doing what you want. But if you are led by the Spirit, you are not subject to the law. Now the works of the flesh are obvious: fornication, impurity, licentiousness, idolatry, sorcery, enmities, strife, jealousy, anger, quarrels, dissensions, factions, envy, drunkenness, carousing, and things like these. I am warning you, as I warned you before: those who do such things will not inherit the kingdom of God.
>
> By contrast, the fruit of the Spirit is love, joy, peace, patience, kindness, generosity, faithfulness, gentleness, and self-control. There is no law against such things. And those who belong to Christ Jesus have crucified the flesh with its passions and desires. If we live by the Spirit, let us also be guided by the Spirit. (Galatians 5:13–25)

That is why Pope John XXIII looked for our age to be a new Pentecost.

CHAPTER FIFTY-FOUR

A WEDDING INVITATION (22:17)

The Spirit and the bride say, "Come."
And let everyone who hears say, "Come."
And let everyone who is thirsty come.
Let anyone who wishes take the water of life as a gift.

Deutero-Isaiah, the anonymous prophet of the Babylonian exile whose profound message was appended to the scroll of Isaiah, tells the broken, beleaguered, desolate people:

Do not fear, for you will not be ashamed;
    do not be discouraged, for you will not suffer disgrace;
for you will forget the shame of your youth,
    and the disgrace of your widowhood you will remember no more.
For your Maker is your husband,
    the LORD of hosts is his name;
the Holy One of Israel is your Redeemer,
    the God of the whole earth he is called.
For the LORD has called you
    like a wife forsaken and grieved in spirit,
like the wife of a man's youth when she is cast off,
    says your God. (Isaiah 54:4–6)

The author of Revelation echoes the marriage analogy to tell us of God's love and the invitation to "hold fast to his covenant" (Exodus 19). Then all who hear that invitation are to echo it and extend it to others. It is an invitation that was also proffered by the anonymous prophet Deutero-Isaiah in the exile:

Ho, everyone who thirsts,
    come to the waters;
and you that have no money,

come, buy and eat!
Come, buy wine and milk
without money and without price.
Why do you spend your money for that which is not bread,
and your labor for that which does not satisfy?
Listen carefully to me, and eat what is good,
and delight yourselves in rich food.
Incline your ear, and come to me;
listen, so that you may live.
I will make with you an everlasting covenant. (Isaiah 55:1–3)

The last line of our text urges us to partake of the gift, which is grace, love and life. The command to partake of it follows the insistent threefold invitation: come, come, come. The Book of Revelation draws to a conclusion with God's invitation to come to grace, to love, to life with himself. All of God's revelation has no other message. It is an invitation with an RSVP attached. He will not accept "no" for an answer. "Listen! I am standing at the door, knocking" (Revelation 3:20).

REFLECTION

Now of that long pursuit
Comes on at hand the bruit;
That voice is round me
like a bursting sea;
'And is thy earth so marred,
Shattered in shard on shard
Lo, all things fly thee for thou fliest Me!
Strange, piteous, futile thing!
Wherefore should any set thee love apart
Seeing none but I makes much of naught'
(He said) 'And human love needs human meriting:
How hast thou merited—
Of all man's clotted clay, the dingiest clot
Alack thou knowest not
How little worthy of any love thou art!

Whom wilt thou find to love ignoble thee,
Save Me, save only Me
All which I took from thee I did but take,
Not for thy harms,
But just that thou might'st seek it in My arms.
All which thy child's mistake fancies as lost,
I have stored for thee at home;
Rise, clasp my hand and come.
Halts by me that footfall:
Is my gloom, after all,
Shade of his hand, outstretched caressingly
'Ah, fondest, blindest, weakest,
I am he whom thou seekest!
Thou dravest love from thee,
who dravest Me.'
(Francis Thompson, "The Hound of Heaven")

CHAPTER FIFTY-FIVE

THY KINGDOM COME (22:18–21)

I warn everyone who hears the words of the prophecy of this book: if anyone adds to them, God will add to that person the plagues described in this book; if anyone takes away from the words of the book of this prophecy, God will take away that person's share in the tree of life and in the holy city, which are described in this book.

The one who testifies to these things says, "Surely I am coming soon."

Amen. Come, Lord Jesus!

The grace of the Lord Jesus be with all the saints. Amen.

The message of this book is to be taken seriously, as a matter of life and death. It concerns eternal life and the "second death." The author uses strong language because he is aware that he lives in critical times. Critical, for us today, means desperate. But in its origin *crisis* means judgment, or requiring a decision. It is a *kairos*, a time of opportunity. Not knowing when Christ will come, the reader can make a judgment like the scoffers of Scripture: "First of all you must understand this, that in the last days scoffers will come, scoffing and indulging their own lusts and saying, 'Where is the promise of his coming? For ever since our ancestors died, all things continue as they were from the beginning of creation!'" (2 Peter 3:3–4)

Or the reader can freeze up, do nothing and just wait, fleeing into a desert (either literal or symbolic), comatosely waiting for the great event. Paul found such ones in Thessalonica,

For even when we were with you, we gave you this command: Anyone unwilling to work should not eat. For we hear that some of you are living in idleness, mere busybodies, not doing any work. Now such persons we command and exhort in the Lord

Jesus Christ to do their work quietly and to earn their own living. Brothers and sisters, do not be weary in doing what is right. (2 Thessalonians 3:10–13)

The fundamentalist preacher who was recently heard to say that preoccupation with ecology was a waste of time since this world would not be around much longer would have been very comfortable among those in Thessalonica who decided to sit it out while waiting for Jesus to come and do his work. Their motto was: "Jesus is coming, stop everything!" They lend credence to the Karl Marx's accusation that "Religion…is the opiate of the people."

The response that is faithful to the gospel, the proper attitude of the true disciple is also given: "…what sort of persons ought you to be in leading lives of holiness and godliness, waiting for and hastening the coming of the day of God?" (2 Peter 3:11–12).

Then they will see "the Son of Man coming in a cloud" with power and great glory. Now when these things begin to take place, stand up and raise your heads, because your redemption is drawing near….Be on guard so that your hearts are not weighed down with dissipation and drunkenness and the worries of this life, and that day does not catch you unexpectedly, like a trap. For it will come upon all who live on the face of the whole earth. Be alert at all times, praying that you may have the strength to escape all these things that will take place, and to stand before the Son of Man. (Luke 21:27–28, 34–36)

The Our Father is a compendium of the themes of the Book of Revelation. It is the eschatological prayer that Christ gave us as a reflection of the attitude that Christians should have "as we wait in joyful hope for the coming of our Savior Jesus Christ."

We say "our" because we are not alone, abandoned or left in isolation. He is with us and unites us into his Son's body, the church.

We say "Father" because we are the brothers and sisters of his son, Jesus who told us that his "Abba" is ours. "He chose us in Christ before the foundation of the world to be holy and blameless before him in love. He destined us for adoption as his children through Jesus Christ" (Ephesians 1:4).

We say "Who art in heaven" from whence he will again send his Son, not because he is the God of ambush theology, but because he still so loves the world (John 3:16).

We say "Hallowed be thy name," Yahweh, the name that is filled with the promise that he is with us; the name we hallow or make holy by entering into his life, saying yes to Jesus, the Way, the Truth and the Life.

We say "Thy Kingdom come" and we cry breathlessly and on tiptoe with the author and his community: "Come, Lord Jesus." The church at Corinth was so impatient that it held on to the original Aramaic of the Jerusalem church: "*Maranatha,*" "Our Lord, come" (1 Corinthians 16:22). We continue that prayer in our acclamations at the consecration of the Mass: "Dying you destroyed our death, rising you restored our life. Lord Jesus, come in glory."

We say "thy will be done on earth as it is in heaven." This will come about when all follow Mary, the first disciple and say: "Be it done unto me according to your word."

We say "Give us this day our daily bread" because only in Jesus, the bread of life, can we find strength to follow him in building up the kingdom of God, by "restoring all things in Christ" (Ephesians 1:10).

We say "Forgive us our trespasses," those things, those idols, that we have preferred to Jesus, to his kingdom, to his gospel.

We say "as we forgive those who trespass against us," for Jesus has helped us to realize that an unforgiving heart is the biggest obstacle to the kingdom: "Father, forgive them for they know not what they do."

We say "And lead us not into temptation," the final struggle that in desperation the powers of evil will wage to try to seize the kingdom from Jesus, who is Lord of lords and King of kings.

Blessed be the God and Father of our Lord Jesus Christ, who has blessed us in Christ with every spiritual blessing in the heavenly places, just as he chose us in Christ before the foundation of the world to be holy and blameless before him in love. He destined us for adoption as his children through Jesus Christ, according to the good pleasure of his will, to the praise of his glorious grace that he freely bestowed on us in the Beloved. In him we have redemption through his blood, the forgiveness of our trespasses, according to the riches of his grace that he lavished on us. With all wisdom and insight he has made known to us the mystery of his will, according to his good pleasure that he set forth in Christ, as a plan for the fullness of time, to gather up all things in him, things in heaven and things on earth. In Christ we have also obtained an inheritance, having been destined according to the purpose of him who accomplishes all things according to his counsel and will, so that we, who were the first to set our hope on Christ, might live for the praise of his glory. In him you also, when you had heard the word of truth, the gospel of your salvation, and had believed in him, were marked with the seal of the promised Holy Spirit; this is the pledge of our inheritance toward redemption as God's own people, to the praise of his glory. (Ephesians 1:3–14)

I bow my knees before the Father, from whom every family in heaven and on earth takes its name. I pray that, according to the riches of his glory, he may grant that you may be strengthened in your inner being with power through his Spirit, and that Christ may dwell in your hearts through faith, as you are being rooted and grounded in love. I pray that you may have the power to comprehend, with all the saints, what is the breadth and length and height and depth, and to know the love of Christ that surpasses knowledge, so that you may be filled with all the fullness of God....

Now to him who by the power at work within us is able to accomplish abundantly far more than all we can ask or imagine, to him be glory in the church and in Christ Jesus to all generations, forever and ever. Amen. (Ephesians 3:15–21)

The literary form known as *apocalyptic* has its own vocabulary that may be unfamiliar and therefore confusing. This is a list of such terms found in this book or others that may be consulted on the topic.

Alleluia or *Halleluia* is a Hebrew word that literally means "Let us praise Yahweh." It is an enthusiastic and joyful invitation to recognize and acclaim the glory of the Lord. (LORD, Hebrew *Adonai*, is used in most Bible versions as a substitute for the Divine Name, Yahweh, which will be occasionally used in this book.)

Anti-Christ designates anyone who opposes and attempts to subvert the lordship of Jesus, the Christ. In the Bible it is found only in the letters of John to apply to those who would deny the real humanity of Jesus. They were the first heretics, known as "Docetists," from the Greek *dokein*, meaning "appear." They maintained that the Son of God only appeared to be human.

Christ comes from the Greek translation of the Hebrew "anointed" or "messiah." Although it became the most common title given to Jesus, he was not comfortable with it because of the connotations it had among his contemporaries. He gave it his own meaning (cf. Luke 4:16ff).

Eschaton comes from the Greek meaning "last" and refers to the period of the final days "when Christ will come again." The study of that time and its accompanying phenomena is called *eschatology*.

Millenerianism refers to the belief of those fundamentalist sects concerning the "1,000 year reign" (cf. chapter forty-eight, *The Thousand Years*). They err by not realizing that the figure is a symbol and not the number of years on a calendar. As a symbol it is one of the most difficult and abstruse in the whole book, and has yet to be interpreted satisfactorily.

Parousia in Greek simply means "arrival" or "coming." In Christian thought it has come to refer to the Second Coming of Jesus. "Dying, you destroyed our death. Rising you restored our life. Lord Jesus, come in glory!" "When we eat this bread and drink this cup, we proclaim your death, Lord Jesus, until you come in glory."

Predestination may simply refer to God's saving plan. But since God is all powerful it has come to refer to the belief that God determines and pre-ordains, and there is nothing we can do about it. In its most difficult formulation it means that even at their creation God planned for some of his creatures to go to heaven, and others to go to hell. In this form it is a denial of free will and leaves no room for reward or punishment. As such, it contradicts everything we know about God and his revelation. But because it is written in the language of a primitive people, Biblical language can easily be misinterpreted as seeming to imply a form of predestination that denies free will.

Rapture comes from the Greek for "caught up." It is used by Paul in 1 Thessalonians 4:17, the very first book of the New Testament: "Then we who are alive, who are left, will be caught up in the clouds together with them to meet the Lord in the air." With this vocabulary and scenario, borrowed from the arrival (parousia) of the emperor, who had come to restore order to a troubled region, Paul symbolically illustrates the Parousia of Jesus. Like the emperor, Jesus will be greeted at his arrival by those "caught up" in enthusiasm. Paul never intended his analogy with the Roman political scene to be taken literally, having the Christians tiptoeing around on the clouds. It is just such a misinterpretation that has occasioned the recently seen bumper sticker: "In case of the rapture, this car will be unoccupied!" Like the word *Anti-Christ*, the word "rapture" is not found in the Book of Revelation referring to Christians, but it has become a part of the eschatological vocabulary.

Yahweh is the name that God revealed to Moses in the burning bush deriving from the verb *to be* in Hebrew.

> Moses said to God, "If I come to the Israelites and say to them, 'The God of your ancestors has sent me to you,' and they ask me, 'What is his name?' what shall I say to them?" God said to Moses, "I AM WHO I AM." He said further, "Thus you shall say to the

Israelites, 'I AM has sent me to you.'" God also said to Moses, "Thus you shall say to the Israelites, 'The LORD, the God of your ancestors, the God of Abraham, the God of Isaac, and the God of Jacob, has sent me to you': This is my name forever, and this my title for all generations." (Exodus 3:13–15)

But later generations, overly literal in the understanding of the first commandment, refrained from using the Name, and where it appeared they substituted LORD (Hebrew: *Adonai*). Later, some confused Christians misunderstood this, and combined the consonants of Yahweh (also spelled with a *J* and means *He Who Is*) with the vowels of *Adonai* (meaning *Lord*) and came up with the fabricated name of Jehovah, which Moses would never recognize. God's name is Yahweh. All modern versions with one exception use the circumlocution "Lord." The *New Jerusalem Bible* uses the sacred name, and it is often used in this book.

BIBLIOGRAPHY

Boring, M. Eugene, *Revelation: A Commentary for Teaching and Preaching* in the Interpretation series, John Knox Press, Knoxville, 1989.

Caird, George B., *The Revelation of Saint John,* Black's New Testament Commentary, Henderson Publishers, Peabody, Mass., 1966.

Collins, Adela Yarbro, *The Apocalypse,* New Jerome Biblical Commentary #63, Prentice Hall, Englewood Cliffs, N.J., 1990.

Fiorenza, Elisabeth Shüssler, *Revelation: Vision of a Just World,* Proclamation Commentaries, 1991.

Harrington, Wilfrid J., *Revelation,* Sacra Pagina Series, Liturgical Press, Collegeville, Minn., 1993.

Metzger, Bruce M., *Breaking the Code: Understanding the Book of Revelation,* Abingdon Press, Nashville, 1993.

Rowland, Christopher J., *Revelation,* New Interpreters' Bible, Abingdon Press, Nashville, 1998.

INDEX